Becoming Peers

Mentoring Girls into Womanhood

Becoming Peers

Mentoring Girls into Womanhood

DeAnna L'am

RED MOON PUBLISHING

Sebastopol, California

Becoming Peers
Mentoring Girls into Womanhood

Copyright © 2006 DeAnna L'am

Red Moon Publishing
P.O. Box 1251, Sebastopol, CA 95473

Orders: www.deannalam.com

Library of congress Control Number: 2007921982

ISBN-13   ISBN-10
978-0-9793518-0-8   0-9793518-0-4

Printed in the United States of America

Cover art:
Ancestral Spirits © by Suzanne deVeuve:
www.suzannedeveuve.com

Cover design by Victoria Temple:
newarts2@sonic.net

Author photograph: Sari Singerman
www.sariphotography.con

Dedicated to ...

My daughter, Ellah Habibti Eva,
Born at home, in water,
October 6, 2000, in Graton, California,
Who, at the age of 6,
Lying on my chest, in the bathtub,
Said, as I poured warm water on her back:
"This feels so good,
I wish I had another Mom here with me,
for you."

To my mother, Eva,
born in Kluj, Transylvania,
February 20, 1929,
who became my friend as Woman
when I turned 18,
who died in Jerusalem, Israel, age 52,
and never met my daughter.

To her mother, my Grandma Serena,
born in Transylvania, September 1904,
whom I called Ika-Trenu, Grandma Train,

who loved me unconditionally
when I was a little girl.
Who died in Jerusalem, Israel, age 92.

To her mother, Rozsa,
my great-grandma,
who was born in Transylvania
and birthed 8 children,
who died with all but two of them
in a concentration camp.
Whose picture I saw
throughout my childhood
hanging on my Grandma's wall.
Who soothed me
during Ellah's birth,
gazing on my closed eyelids
from her place at the altar
by the hearth.

To her mother, and her's,
whose names I never knew.

To my mother's line,
and the lines of all our mothers...

Acknowledgments

My deepest gratitude goes to my husband and companion, Julian Shaw, for his steady fire of heart and hearth, and for his continuous support, in ways both visible and invisible.

I am grateful to my daughter's kindergarten teacher, Kate O'Brien, in whose capable hands I daily entrusted Ellah, as I wrote this book, knowing she was safe, nurtured, and cared for deeply.

My heartfelt gratitude goes to Tamara Slayton, who no longer walks this earth, for her pioneering vision and work, and for her menstrual cloth products, which were my point of entry into this empowering journey.

I hold much joyful appreciation for my kindred spirits overseas, Nira Carmel and Amir Carmel, who profoundly inspired me when they bravely charted the unknown terrain of Eldering, creating egalitarian seasonal circles in which adults thrive to model integrity of spirit to the young in their midst.

I offer deep thanks to Marguerite Rigoglioso, editor extraordinaire, whose insight, perceptions, and suggestions helped greatly expand the scope and advance the quality of this book.

I extend heartfelt appreciation to Joan Morais for her encouragement, invaluable advice, and support during the publication process of this book.

I am grateful to my dear friend Marta Quest for her meticulous and professional proofreading of the manuscript in its final stages. Namasté.

And finally, my gratitude goes to all of the girls and women around the world who entrusted me with their stories, their tears, and their joys. Without you this book never would have been possible!

Table of Contents

I. Journeying

Returning to the moon:
My own journey

My consciousness as Woman wasn't truly raised until I left Israel, my country of origin. I was 28 years old and eager to start an adventurous life in London.

Years of involvement in women's activities in England, and subsequently in the United States, had me swimming in female consciousness, from the political to the spiritual. The circles of women in which I participated shared tears and laughter, histories of struggle, of loss, of overcoming abuse, and of recovery. We even compared stories of how we "lost" our virginity, and yet, *not once* was our menstrual blood mentioned -- the taboo being so deeply ingrained, we didn't even suspect we had left anything uncovered.

I first encountered a different view of menstrual blood while traveling with my partner in Northern California. Living in Southern California at the time, we heard of "the north" being a different land with a different kind of consciousness. On our journey, we stopped at a health-food store in the small town of Calistoga. I was browsing a pamphlet rack when my eyes fell on a booklet called Woman Kind, written by Tamara Slayton. It talked about menstrual cloth pads and had a testimonial from a woman who said she had started liking her periods after getting used to cloth pads. "Yeah, right!" I thought to myself. But the story and the cloth pads were to stick in my memory.

Not long afterward, I came across the work of Kisma Stepanich, another strong advocate for the reclaiming of women's menstrual power. In her book Sister Moon Lodge, I encountered the cloth pads again, emerging as a shy yet persistent new friend who didn't want to be forgotten.

I resolved to take the plunge!

I started by making a bag for covering a "Moon Bowl" in which I would soak my pads. Preparing for my next period, I found a beautiful deep-red velvet cloth. I cut out a large circle, punched holes around its circumference, and threaded the holes with a rich golden ribbon to create a drawstring bag.

Not having a proper lidded "Moon Bowl," I pulled the biggest glass bowl I could find from my kitchen cupboard, filled it with water, covered it with a plate, and placed it on top of the velvet circle, drawing the string up and around to enclose it. The effect was stunning: a three-dimensional half-sphere of plush, velvety red now sat on my bathroom counter, trimmed with gold, and sparkling in the sunlight coming through the window. My period had not come yet, but I began to eagerly await it as never before.

I bought some brand new Moon Pads, made of organic cotton, and thought about the message of "cleanliness" my mother had conveyed to me when my menarche -- my first menstruation -- arrived. She never told me that my menstrual blood was "dirty," but she surely emphasized the need to clean, wash, and hide my blood and pads from view. I understood her unspoken words: my blood was foul and I was supposed to conceal any evidence of its presence, dispose of it quickly, wash myself often, and pretend it wasn't there.

In preparing my Moon Bowl for my next menstrual period, I suddenly realized I would need to touch my blood. This was new. Years of disposing of menstrual products had made the blood synonymous with trash. Yet my research had suggested a reverse concept: my blood, our collective blood as menstruating women, was sacred. It was made of the substance that nourishes life. For what is menstrual blood if not the tissue grown by our wombs in preparation for pregnancy, in anticipation of new life? Our body sheds this life-giving, precious substance every month we do not conceive. This blood can alternatively fulfill its purpose by becoming rich, nourishing fertilizer for the plants in our homes and gardens, or it can be thrown to the trash in disgust. I was standing at the threshold of making a new choice about what to do with my menstrual blood, one that was different from what I'd been doing for years.

I found myself worrying about the odor of my blood bothering me. Although I had read that the smell typically associated with menstrual blood was in fact the result of the blood's reaction with bleach and other chemicals infused in paper menstrual products, I wasn't sure. Years' worth of odor still lingered in my visceral memory; I was somewhat torn. All I could do was wait for what discoveries might come.

When my menstrual flow finally came that month, I welcomed it with a cloth pad and a new attitude. Changing a cloth pad was a different experience. For the first time, I was really curious about my blood. It struck me as odd that I had never had such curiosity before. Was it because my mom's sterile explanations at Menarche had wiped out any sense of mystery?

I was curious about the sight, the texture, the smell, and the feel of my blood. I approached it initially with a mixture of resistance and fascination. The most surprising sensation I experienced in using the new pads was that of *flow*. I realized that when I was "corked" with a tampon, the flow had been halted at source. Yet now, allowed to freely emerge, my blood was flowing from me in a way that drew my awareness. As I walked in the world, I felt as though I had a secret spring between my legs.

The Sanskrit word for vagina is "Yoni," which translates as "Divine Passage" or "Sacred Space." I wondered about the relationship between "secret" and "sacred," for the current that was flowing from me felt like both. A secret, sacred spring was streaming out of me and it felt alive! I didn't expect to feel so moved by it. It reminded me of a sensation after lovemaking: that of a river flowing from me, a feeling I always cherished.

When it came time to change my pad, I gingerly approached the task. The sight of my blood was somewhat different than I had expected, given that I had never really taken the time to look before. The crimson patch was odorless, just as I had read! I slowly drew open the golden ribbon of the plush bag that enclosed my Moon Bowl, and the red velvet slid down around it to rest on my bathroom counter. Under the kitchen plate a still body of water sat like a mini homemade clear lake. I immersed my cloth pad, and the water started slowly changing to pink, then red. The effect reminded me of watercolors. I played for a while with my hands in the red water, transported back to kindergarten, when getting wet and messy was fun!

The water turned darker red. I began reflecting on the nutrients that were held in the bowl, which reflected back to me my firm decision (thus far) to not have a child; the choice to use my skills, instead, to benefit my community rather than raise a human being. I realized how very magical my body was in its capacity to do either one.

That evening, I returned to my covered Moon Bowl, where the water had continued to draw sacred blood from my cloth pad. As I wrung out the pad, I realized this day marked the first time I had handled my own internal substance, my own life blood; it felt empowering. I was doing something that millions of women around the world had done throughout time, by rivers, oceans, and lakes. I was taking charge of my cyclicity, reclaiming it from the hands of billion-dollar corporations. I started laughing out loud when it dawned on me that I would never again need to run out to the store at the last minute for tampons!

This life-giving substance in which my hands were playing was my own fertilizing nectar. I wasn't going to discard it as dirty, unwanted "bodily discharge." I realized that giving it to my houseplants would become an act symbolic of fertilizing my projects in the larger world, of nurturing all that I had planted into its full growth and fruition. I ceremonially carried my crimson-filled bowl to my leafy ficus plant. Carefully pouring red water onto the potted soil, I felt like a mother feeding her child. A couple of cycles later I could see the results, unmistakably staring at me: my houseplants were ecstatic! They shot up, and leafed-out happier and healthier than I'd ever seen them. My cycle had come full circle: my blood was nourishing life wherever it touched it.

Journeying
Why this book?

When adult women tell girls who have started their menstrual cycle that they have "become women," what do they mean? What does it mean to "become a woman"?

Legally, a girl's status doesn't change once she starts menstruating. She is not allowed to drive a vehicle or consume alcohol, and even though her body is now able to conceive a child, she is still at too tender an age to engage in sexual activities. What has really changed? How is she "a girl no more"? Are we simply paying lip service to the idea that menstruation means the start of womanhood?

I believe that in order for a girl's menstruation to serve as a meaningful entry into womanhood, it is *essential* that her mother, and other women in her life, transform their relationships with her. This is a call to mothers, women relatives, or women family friends of a girl about to undergo her miraculous bodily transformation, to learn how to become friends and equals with the girl in their life. It is up to *you* to learn how to mentor her

19

into, eventually, becoming your peer. This book provides guidelines for how you may go about this momentous and rewarding process together. In order to address birth mothers, as well as other women who wish to step into a girl's life in a mentoring capacity, I refer throughout this book to our young as "girls" rather than "daughters."

Whether we are a girl's biological mother, a relative, or a friend, the first step for us as women is to "get our own house in order," so to speak; to clear out and cleanse anything that might prevent us from properly being able to welcome our girl to womanhood. Usually this entails going on a journey. Often it is a deeply healing one.

My own journey from seeing menstruation as "the curse" to feeling personally empowered by my menstrual period and all it represents, was a profoundly healing voyage. The more empowered I felt, the more I noticed women around me thirsting for such empowerment. Excited to share my learning journey with others, I called together a women's menstrual circle at a metaphysical bookstore near my home at the time in Southern California. The evening astounded me: a large group of women bonded immediately when, without hesitation, they each began recalling the stories of their first menstruation. These stories, which they had never shared with anyone, stunned us all in their similarity.

This is when I first realized that the syndrome of shame-ignorance-pain-fear-embarrassment regarding menstruation is not only prevalent, it is the norm. It soon became clear that any feelings of empowerment or moments of celebration were rare, at least for women of my generation who had come of age in the late 1960s and early 1970s. (And teachers I have met around the world since then, ranging from elementary school to university-level faculty, have been informing me that things may not have changed that much for some young women of the subsequent generations: many of their students still report associating shame, fear, or embarrassment with their periods.)

I started holding Red Moon circles aimed at helping women welcome the younger generation -- their daughters, relatives, or other girls -- into womanhood. Since I began this work, I have sat in circles of girls and women around the world. In them, women have uniformly shared the wounds they have experienced in transitioning out of maidenhood. Yet, at the same time, most have been in a hurry to skip over their own negative experiences and "make things perfect" for their daughters or other younger girls. It has become clear to me, however, that by carrying around their own personal and collective shame about menarche and menstruation, women are hampered in their ability to celebrate girls' rites of passage with grace, ease, and creativity. They are eager but embarrassed; they don't know how to approach such a celebration, or they become overbearing about it and find their daughters unwilling to participate. This is not surprising, given that we have no cultural models for Coming of Age celebrations.

These experiences brought me to the realization that women need to heal *their own* wounds of maidenhood before they can be fully present for their girls' ceremonies.

Sitting in these circles, I noticed something else of great importance, as well. Although younger girls were initially hesitant to talk about menstruation, in general they did not possess quite the degree of shame about the subject that their mothers did. This enabled them to be effective witnesses for the stories of their mothers and other elder women in the group. By serving as witnesses, the girls themselves were transformed into healers for the women of the older generations. This put them into an immediate "peer" relationship with all women in the circle, regardless of their age.

Thus the honest and straightforward sharing elevated relationships between mothers and daughters, women and adolescent girls. The generations were no longer bound in power relations, where the younger party was inevitably in a "one-down" position. Rather, mothers and daughters, women-elders and girls, became friends and equals. This led to the conception of this book, which has been birthed to provide mothers, and women at large, with the tools for becoming peers to their daughters or to girls in their life, once menarche arrives.

This book is a resource for mothers, stepmothers, grandmothers, aunts, big sisters, cousins, and any woman who cares about a girl who is Coming of Age in her community. Regardless of your biological relationship to the girl you mentor, it is the integrity with which you model womanhood that will nurture the bond between you.

This book starts with you: a woman healing her own maidenhood wounds, and making peace with her power. Healing a wound of the heart is best attained in a sacred ceremonial space. Our hearts and souls speak in images rather than words, and a good ceremony creates potent and poignant images to counter the wounding.

The book thus first illuminates what a ceremony is. It goes on to outline elements of ceremony, and then presents examples of rite-of-passage ceremonies ranging from those designed to help you heal the maidenhood wound, to those that will assist you in welcoming girls into womanhood. It aims to help you move through the transition from Mother to Peer, from Elder to Equal. And it guides you through the Coming of Age year as a process of transformation for both yourself and your daughter or the young girl in your life.

This book aspires to shift the cultural paradigm that views menstruation as a pest, nuisance, bother, annoyance, irritant, and, ultimately, a curse. Not only is it intended *to help people see menstruation as an empowering experience, it aims to create a shift in the way mothers and daughters, women and girls, relate to one another. It strives to assist them in using the very pivotal time when a girl's body changes from a child's to a woman's -- as an opportunity to develop a deeper, more authentic, more satisfying, and more joyful relationship with one another.*

II. Healing and Celebrating

Creating ceremony

Ceremony is a means of giving form to our intentions.

Whether we wish to express gratitude, draw on inner strength, ask for guidance, bring a vision into reality, or mark a milestone, our intentions often become more powerful when we give them an external expression. Such expression allows an intention to move from a thought in our mind into manifested reality.

Our psyche doesn't differentiate between "real" or "imagined" events. It simply responds to whatever thoughts we generate. If, for example, I am home alone at night and hear a movement outside, I might immediately imagine that an intruder is present, and that will cause my whole being to contract with fear. A moment later, I may realize that the sound was caused by a cat in my back yard. The external reality isn't the important issue here; I have still experienced the same emotional and physical state as if there had been an actual intruder. The more important point is that our psyche will respond equally to all experiences, whether externally or internally generated.

With ceremony, we are creating an *internally generated* event that will be experienced by our psyche and emotional body as a lived reality. Ceremony is thus a powerful tool for both reaching back to heal past wounds and looking ahead to bring forth new visions. In the timeless space of ceremony, all is in the present tense, and everything becomes possible.

We begin the creation of ceremony with an intention. One such intention might be to honor our femininity; another, to celebrate our girl's Coming of Age. We then move to develop the activities, which will give that intention form; thus we begin designing the various parts of our ceremony. What does this process look like?

Moving from Intention to Action

Sit down in a quiet place to find the silence inside yourself. Let the Earth support your posture, let go of tense muscles in your shoulders, back, or neck. Exhale, releasing anything that doesn't belong to this quiet moment. Inhale strength from the Earth beneath you as though you are breathing it through your whole body. Place your attention, and your own soothing palm, on your heart area. Allow an intention regarding your own Menarche experience to form there. Ask yourself a question such as:

* How would I have liked my mother to welcome me into womanhood?

* If I could have had the first day of my bleeding be exactly the way I wanted it, what would it have looked like?

* If I could have had more women involved in my adolescent years, who would they have been? What would they have said to me?

Accept the first thought or image that comes to mind without changing it.

Look at the intention that surfaced within you, and ask yourself how it could be translated into form. What visual object, gesture, action, or symbol would best express it? What would your intention look like if it were three-dimensional? If it were dressed, what would it wear? How would you like to *feel* as you experience your intention coming alive? What action would create such a feeling? What ambience, clothing, props, and acts would facilitate it?

This exercise should provide you with some initial ideas for how you might "stage" a ceremony that will help you bring your intention into form regarding both your own healing as well as your girl's menarche celebration. We will return to this activity in the section entitled "Healing and celebrating the maiden within" on page 53.

For now, keep in mind that the best way to approach ceremony is from the perspective of the open, eager, and bold young girl that you once were. Think back to your childhood. What was it like playing with your dolls, your stuffed animals, or perhaps your toy cars and trucks? Do you remember creating elaborate scenarios and adventures for them with your friends? Let the same joy and abandon possess you when creating ceremony as you experienced when you played with your toys, climbed trees, delved into books, walked in nature, and impressed your wild visions upon the world. Allow that inner girl to guide you. And remember that now you also have your hard-earned adult wisdom to add to the mix, which will enable you to create a truly grand adventure!

The next chapter, "Elements of ceremony," will outline the structure of a ceremony. Specific guidance on how to create various ceremonies related to the theme of this book will follow in the chapters entitled "Our mothers' line," "Healing and celebrating the maiden within," "Circle activities for mothers and daughters, women and girls," and "Welcoming girls into womanhood." Take time to read them, let the images wash over you, and allow your intuition to guide you in the creation of your own ceremonies.

Healing and Celebrating
Elements of ceremony

Ceremonial space is sacred, and sacred space is extra-ordinary. The regular, day-to-day business doesn't belong here. It is a time and space for speaking and listening from the heart. No chit-chat is allowed! This is a place for confiding, for exploring vulnerable areas within ourselves while witnessing and supporting one another. It is a place to enjoy an authentic bond as circle peers.

A ceremonial circle can have as few as two participants, or as many as you desire. Ceremonies, like plays, have a beginning, a middle, and an end. The beginning and end take us from the everyday, mundane reality into sacred space, and back again. The middle is where the magic is allowed to unfold.

Magic can only unfold freely if there is a strong sense of safety among all participants in the circle. A crucial element of any group ceremony is _confidentiality_. Words spoken, feelings expressed, and stories shared all need to be kept close to participants' hearts, and should never be disclosed outside the boundaries of the circle. Confidentiality allows for confiding. It creates a safe container in which trust may grow. Before starting your ceremony, take a few moments to establish a confidentiality agreement among all of the women in your circle. My own preferred way is to ask the group if they are willing to agree that anything said within the circle remains confidential. Be clear that women may freely talk about their *own* experiences outside the circle, but that they must omit names, or anything shared by others, that *led* to their inner experience.

This section of the book will discuss the basic elements of ceremony. If you're already experienced in conducting ceremony, you may just want to skim this part and jump to the section entitled "Our mothers' line." If you're new to ceremony, the following will provide some guidance on how to stage the more elaborate ceremonies to come, and hopefully it will continue to spark new ideas for how you can make such events your own.

The invocation

How do we establish the ceremony as a time and place apart from the ordinary world? One way is by announcing it! Think back to the girl within; allow yourself to remember *how you made things exactly so simply by pronouncing them to be so (and fully believing in your proclamation!). This is what is known, in the ceremonial world, as the Invocation. We state an intention, and our reality becomes that which we have announced it to be. An invocation sets what you are doing apart from your daily activities; it establishes sacred space. It moves the group from a state of chatter and scatter to one of focus.*

Invocations can be performed verbally or musically. Choose what feels best to you. To start your ceremony, you may want to ring a bell, sing a song, or state your intentions reciting poetry or simple words.

Here are a few sample invocations (ranging from simple to more elaborate):

- *Thank you, everyone, for being here. I would like to start with a moment of silence, to mark the beginning of our ceremony.*

- *Let's hold hands in a circle and allow ourselves to take a few deep breaths together.*

- *I call upon the strength of Mother Earth to fill our circle, to ground us and hold us.*

- *Let's close our eyes and feel our feet firmly on the ground. Placing our attention on the soles of our feet, let's send our roots deep into Mother Earth. With our exhales, let's breathe out anything that doesn't belong to this moment, such as our work day, the rush to get here, the traffic on the way. Let's exhale anything that doesn't serve us, such as our internal judgments, our opinions about ourselves falling short, or any form of guilt; let the weight of it all dissolve, and feel how much lighter we are without it. With our inhales, let's breathe in the freshness of this moment, Now. Let's take a few deep breaths together, inhaling freshness, exhaling what we want to release. When you are ready, bring yourself fully into the present and gently open your eyes.*

Another common invocation addresses the four elements/directions. Indigenous traditions all over the world associate the four elements of Earth, Fire, Water, and Air with the four directions: East, South, West, and North (with some variations as to which goes with which, depending on the tradition and the location).

The four elements/directions are considered in these traditions to be literal sources of energy and strength, and a means by which one may connect with Spirit. Indigenous ceremonies typically start with invoking the four elements/directions, and end with thanking them. Beginning a ceremony in this way is often referred to as "casting the circle," because it involves essentially moving one's attention in a 360-degree arc around the group. This is just another way of naming the process of separating sacred space from everyday reality. Once "cast," the circle in which the group is held becomes a symbolic container for supporting participants' union with Spirit.

As mentioned before, there are slight variations as to which elements are associated with which cardinal directions. In this book, I use the system based on the European oral tradition into which I was initiated. In this tradition, Earth is associated with East, Fire with South, Water with West, and Air with North. However, if you already have your own tradition, or if you feel intuitively called to change the associations (particularly according to the specifics of your own geographical location), it is absolutely fine, as long as all four elements/directions are honored.

An invocation to the four elements is typically done by facing each direction in turn, starting with the East, and turning clockwise. This rotation is considered to bring energy into the circle. Here is a sample script of an invocation to the four elements. These words are spoken aloud. One person may invoke all of the directions, or you may assign each direction to a different person, as you see fit. If you are already familiar with the qualities of each direction and element, you may feel free to improvise:

(The invoker, or the entire group, turns to face East): Spirit of **Earth,** come be with us now! As the sun rises anew every morning, so may we be renewed with every step we take. May we be deeply rooted in Mother Earth, yet tread lightly, leaving beauty behind us. Let us ground in your depth and grow tall, bearing the sweet fruits of our labor. Spirit of Earth, come be with us now and bless our circle.

*(Facing South): Spirit of **Fire**, come be with us now! Place of our desire, our passion and compassion, let your flames rekindle the fire in our belly; ignite the blaze of our creativity; let the torch of our inner guidance illumine our way. Spirit of Fire, come be with us now and bless our circle.*

*(Facing West): Spirit of **Water**, come be with us now! Let the cup of our loving wash over us. Oceans of our emotions, teach us to flow as water, always finding the path of least resistance; let us delve into our depths and find answers in our dreams. Spirit of Water, come be with us now and bless our circle.*

*(Facing North): Spirit of **Air**, come be with us now! Winds of change, help us sweep the cobwebs from the corners of our mind. Show us the world through a bird's eye. Let us soar on wings of inspiration, let our imagination fly! Spirit of Air, come be with us now and bless our circle.*

Whichever method you use to start, repeat it at the end, so that your ceremonial time is framed as something extraordinary that stands outside of the mundane, routine world. Remember that it is more powerful to speak or musically intone your invocations *standing up*. You may even choose to raise your arms, creating a symbolic chalice with your body. Assuming a chalice-like stance creates an energetic opening through which you are inviting strength to pour in as you embody your intention. You may find other postures that are powerful to you. Let yourself experiment, and only do what feels comfortable.

A ceremony can be solitary or communal, planned or spontaneous. In a solitary ceremony, you may choose to be silent throughout, speaking your invocations and intentions inwardly; or you may wish to voice them out loud. The suggestions in this book, however, pertain mostly to group ceremonies, as they usually call for advanced planning.

The body of your ceremony

This is the heart, and the longest part of a ceremony, where you creatively give form to your intentions. You will want to prepare this part carefully, according to the kind of ceremony you are designing: Coming of Age, Affirming your Womanhood, and so forth. To read more about such ceremonies, and to get specific ideas for the body of various ceremonies, look in the sections of this book entitled "Our mothers' line" (page 44), "Healing and celebrating the maiden within" (page 53), "Circle activities for mothers and daughters, women and girls" (page 84), and "Welcoming girls into womanhood" (page 119). Remember that the clearer you are about your intentions, and about what you wish to achieve, the more focused your ceremony will be. Whatever you do, make sure it is meaningful to you.

The closing of your ceremony

As mentioned earlier, just as it is important to open your ceremony properly so as to establish sacred space, so it is important to close appropriately in order to help the group make a smooth transition to their ordinary lives. The closing should mirror your opening in terms of style.

A few examples of circle closings
(Ranging from simple to more elaborate):

• Thank you, everyone, for participating. I would like to close with a moment of silence, to mark the ending of our ceremony.

- Let's hold hands in a circle and allow ourselves to take a few deep breaths together, to close our circle.

- Let's close our eyes and feel our feet firmly on the ground. Let's exhale together, affirming all that we have let go of today to be indeed gone, feeling ourselves lighter without all that we have ceremonially released. With our inhales, let's breathe in gratitude for our time together. Let's take a few deep breaths in this way. When you are ready, bring yourself fully into this moment, and gently open your eyes.

- I thank Mother Earth, who filled our circle, grounded us, and held us.

If you invoked the four elements/directions at the beginning of your ceremony, you are obliged to close by thanking and releasing them. Similarly to the invocation, closing the circle is done facing each direction in turn, starting with the East. However this time the turning is done counter-clockwise, which is the rotation considered to release energy from the circle and let it go. Here is an example of a script for such a closing. As you will note, this kind of circle closing is typically shorter than the opening invocation to the four elements/directions. Again, if you are familiar with this kind of closing, you may feel free to improvise:

> (The invoker, or the entire group, faces East): Gratitude, spirit of **Earth**! We sense your presence with every step we take. May we always be connected to you. We say hail and farewell!
>
> (Facing North): Thank you, spirit of **Air**, for the renewal we have experienced today! May we always glide on your gentle currents. We say hail and farewell!
>
> (Facing West): Gratitude, spirit of **Water**! Our hearts are full and flowing, may we always drink deeply! We say hail and farewell!
>
> (Facing South): Thank you, spirit of **Fire**, for igniting our passion and our compassion! May your flames always burn steady to illumine our way! We say hail and farewell!

The circle is open but never broken. Merry meet, and merry part, and merry meet again!

Now that you have a sense of the basic structure of a ceremony, it is up to you to sculpt its body, to clothe, embellish, and adorn it. Again, you will find ideas and guidelines in the following chapters: "Our mothers' line," "Healing and celebrating the maiden within," "Circle activities for mothers and daughters, women and girls," and "Welcoming girls into womanhood." Remember your most intuitive guide -- the girl within -- and let her playful memories of dolls, nature, and make-believe show you the way.

Healing and Celebrating
Our mothers' line

"I am DeAnna, daughter of Eva, daughter of Serena, daughter of Rozsa, daughter of Mother Earth.

"I am DeAnna, mother of Ellah."

So starts one of the most simple yet moving ways of introducing ourselves in a group of women. We have come into this world through a woman's body, and our cells and souls carry the memory of her within, even if we never had the opportunity to know her.

We are connected to all women who ever walked this Earth. Like them, we cycle monthly. We may have much, or nothing, in common with our mothers and grandmothers; we may be separated by culture, religion, and generation gaps, yet we all cycle. We share this intimate experience, whether we have spoken of it together or not.

Recognizing our bond as cycling women makes us peers. Yet this may be something neither we nor our mothers and grandmothers have come to acknowledge. Whether we hardly speak to one another or have the warmest of relationships, how many of us have come to the point where we consider ourselves peers with the elder women in our families or in our lives? How many of us have emerged from the mother-daughter dynamic to stand, side by side, as equals?

Yet, in cycling, we are one. As cycling women we are no longer confined by roles or by hierarchy. We are all souls in a woman's body, aligned with the moon and tides, bleeding and catching our blood monthly, conceiving children or choosing not to. Through our extraordinary blood we are all made equal; we stand in the image of the first, archetypal Woman.

We share our cyclicity with *all* women -- past, present, and future. When we call the names of our mothers, grandmothers, and foremothers, as far back as we can, we invoke our *mothers' line*. This is the line of hearts and wombs that birthed us forth -- and it was their cycling that made birthing possible. Invoking our mothers' line allows us to connect with our female ancestors on a different level, whether they still live or *whether they have crossed over. It reminds us that we are not alone. It lets us know that there is a line of women behind us who cycled and commiserated together; who loved and conceived; who birthed, miscarried, or aborted children; who nursed and raised a line of daughters. It affirms the never-ending chain in which we each are a living link. How reassuring it is to know that we can call upon this lineage for spiritual guidance!*

Our mothers' line also extends forward, into the future. Our daughters are the newest living link in this ever-expanding chain. They, too, will grow to honor the line from which they sprang forth if we model to them the importance and sacredness of it in our own lives.

By honoring our female lineage and passing the legacy on to our daughters, we reclaim a timeless connection and strengthen a deep sense of belonging. This is what allows us to blossom and thrive as women.

Healing and Celebrating
Our mothers' line:
A sample ceremony

This ceremony is intended for a group of women, or a mixed group of women and girls. It is easy to perform, and can be enormously meaningful to both novices and seasoned ceremonialists. I am always moved by how deeply women resonate with this simple yet powerful circle activity.

You will need:

- *A ball of red/crimson yarn*
- *A candle in a holder*
- *A pair of scissors*
- *A simple altar: a space that focuses your attention and intention, placed either in the center of your circle (indoors/outside), or centrally around your circle (indoors/outdoors). Adorn it with objects that, to you, symbolize your femininity and beauty. These may include: a beautiful cloth; pictures of yourself, your mother, grandmother, or other women ancestors; images of the Feminine; jewelry; statues; a crystal or*

rock; flowers; other elements from nature; and so forth.
• A verbal confidentiality agreement to be established prior to starting the ceremony.
• A comfortable sitting arrangement, such as pillows, back-jacks, and the like. These could be provided by you, or by each participant (with advance notice).

The invocation

Please refer to the section of this book entitled "Elements of ceremony" on page 32, to choose an invocation that suits your needs, or, if you are comfortable doing so, create your own invocation.

The body of your ceremony

Holding a big ball of crimson yarn, mindfully wrap the end around your left (heart's) wrist a few times while you speak your name, the names of your mother, grandmother, and the women of your mother's line as far back as you can, ending with Mother Earth. Continue by reciting the names of your daughters, stepdaughters, heart-daughters, or granddaughters, if you have them. For example: "I am DeAnna, daughter of Eva, daughter of Serena, daughter of Rozsa, daughter of Mother Earth. I am DeAnna, mother of Ellah."

When you are finished invoking your mothers' line, hand the ball of yarn to the woman on your left. Without cutting the cord, and leaving some loose yarn between you, she should proceed to wrap her left (heart's) wrist while invoking her own maternal ancestors, and any daughters or granddaughters. Pass the red yarn around the entire circle, allowing each woman to invoke and wrap.

When the yarn comes full circle back to you, it will become evident that a red thread connects you all. This serves as a visual symbol of the bloodline that unites you with all women who ever lived, and ever will live, on our Mother Earth.

Linked by the red thread in this way, you may want to sing or chant. You might even start moving around your space in a snaking motion, spiraling toward the center and out again. Such a dance allows you to sense your literal connection with each other, and demonstrates your ability to synchronize differences into a unity of celebration. If you feel comfortable, let your singing and dancing build in energy and rise to a crescendo.

At this point, you will sense that your energy has culminated. Together, the group should instinctively allow the singing and dancing to wind down, and you should come to a point of silence, with each of you standing or sitting back in your original places.

You may choose to close the ceremony now, or continue to add other elements to it. You will find ideas for this in the chapters "Healing and celebrating the maiden within" (page 53), "Circle activities for mothers and daughters, women and girls" (page 84), and "Welcoming girls into womanhood" (page 119).

If your ceremony has come to completion, it is time to close the circle. Instruct the women to break off (or cut with scissors) the yarn between them all, and to wrap the excess around their wrists. Then have women help each other tie the ends on their neighbors' wrists so that they remain wearing the yarn as a bracelet of sorts. It is practically impossible to tie a knot around one's own wrist, so this provides an opportunity for each woman to experience her interdependence with both her peers in the circle and her ancestors.

Recommend that the women wear their red wristband for a certain period of time as a sacred reminder of their connection to the group, to their mothers' line, and to all women.

You may suggest that women wear the red "bracelet" until their next Moon Time, until the next full moon, for some other specified period, or for as long as they wish. You can reassure them that yarns of various materials are able to withstand many showers without breaking. Be sure to remind them to cut off their wristband with intention, when the time comes. They may want to spend a moment remembering their ceremony and what the band symbolizes. They may also want to "give it back" to Mother Earth by burying or planting it under a beautiful plant. In that way it will serve as a constant reminder of their connection to all cycling women.

The closing
Please refer to the section of this book entitled "Elements of ceremony," starting on

page 32, to find a way for closing your circle, or create your own. Note that it is always important to mark the closing so as to allow everyone to make the psychological transition to ordinary space as smoothly as possible.

A shared feast always adds to the festivities!

Healing and Celebrating
Healing and celebrating the maiden within

Women and girls have sat together in circles since time immemorial.

The eagerness with which women around the world have read _The Red Tent_ by Anita Diamant is a testament to how hungry women are for sitting together in circles, for sharing and acknowledging our Moon Time, and for being honored as women. Participating in contemporary Moon Circles, women experience both sadness and excitement. The sadness arises from the deep sense of loss we feel over the ways in which women's bodies, rhythms, and needs have been disregarded and denigrated throughout "modern" history. The excitement arises from the possibilities we sense emerging as we recall a distant past when women's ways and women's blood were honored. The picture Diamant has offered of how women may have once communed together nourishes us on a cellular level -- and makes us crave more!

I often hear women say that reading a book is not enough, that we need to make these new/old ways of being once more a part of our culture. Yet I also sense women's despair at the thought of trying to change an entire culture. For many, the task just seems too daunting, and thus they don't take any action. Rather, they continue to bear their lot, often fluctuating from feeling angry and resentful to feeling depressed and hopeless.

Cultures may be slow to change, yet a women has the power to transform her own life overnight. All she need do is call a woman friend and arrange a meeting with sacred intent. She can also call together a few women friends -- and their daughters -- for a sacred circle. This is how a cultural shift is started!

It's really that easy. We can't sit around and wait for the "culture" to change so that our girls will be properly welcomed into womanhood. We need to be the change we want to see happen; it is our responsibility to do so. We have the power to create our own models, and we can look to images of other eras and epochs in history for guidance. In actively creating the culture we want to live in, one step at a time, we inspire our girls and daughters, our granddaughters, and their daughters to follow in our footsteps.

Our ancestors and our children are calling us to become Elders. They are calling us to excavate, reclaim, create, conjure, and invent traditions for honoring Womanhood and welcoming girls into our midst.

What stops us, again, are the wounds we ourselves experienced when we were not honored as we transitioned from girlhood to womanhood. Our stories of shame, embarrassment, pain, ridicule, fear, or sheer ignorance need to be heard and released. In order to truly welcome our girls, we must first welcome ourselves. We must reclaim our own lost Rite of Passage and celebrate it, now.

Someone once said it is never too late to have a happy childhood. It is also never too late to have a Rite of Passage! The sometimes painful facts of our own personal and collective history need not stand in the way of our healing and of our celebrating the girl within.

The first step is to get re-acquainted with her.

Reconnecting with your Inner Maiden

Take a moment and close your eyes. Call forth the Maiden you once were. Remember how it felt to be a young girl, on the verge of womanhood. What were you looking forward to? What bodily changes did you eagerly await -- or did you perhaps feel some apprehension about? Once your menses, your period, came, how do you wish you had been celebrated -- in that hour, that day, that week? What kind of reassurance do you wish you had received? Who would you have wanted to attend your Coming of Age ceremony? Your mother? Grandmothers? Sisters? Cousins? Aunts? Best friend? Family friends? Classmates? What do you wish your mother had said to you? The adult women in your clan? Your girlfriends?

Write down these words in simple lines, poems, or stories.

After you have written down your ideas, you may want to look to poetry books for further inspiration. When you have polished your words to your satisfaction, set a date and invite your women -- blood family and heart family -- all of those with whom you truly feel safe and by whom you feel truly loved. There is no one who "should" be invited. This is an event where you get to make the guest list based solely on the way you feel about those you invite, and in this case only good feelings count!

The date could be a full moon, which will shine on your circle and imbue it with its energy, if you conduct your ceremony outside after dark. It could be your birthday, or any date that feels empowering to you. Your circle may take place in the morning, dusk, or at night, at any location, indoors or outdoors. This is *your* Rite of Passage, and the most important thing is that it be designed to make you feel supported, embraced, and honored.

It's a good idea to choose a special Mistress of Ceremonies to be the one "welcoming you to womanhood" in the rite. This could be a family member or a friend. You will want to plan the event with this person and be sure to communicate to her the inner pictures and images you hold about how you would like the ceremony to feel to you. You may want to ask her to be the one who speaks to you the words you have written, the words you wish your mother had said to you. Imagine how profoundly healing this will be for you! Envision how receptive you will be, after all these years, to take-in the message you have been longing to hear, perhaps without even knowing it.

You also may want to consider having your Mistress of Ceremonies be your mother herself, if she is alive and available. Your first assumption may be that your mother would not be open to something like this, or that having her in this role would not be appropriate. But you may be surprised to learn how much her own inner maiden is in need of healing, as she, too, has never been celebrated. Consider taking a risk and inviting her, while trusting your instincts about what ultimately feels right for you.

<u>Healing and Celebrating</u>
The maiden within:
A sample ceremony

This ceremony is intended for you and a circle of women you love and trust. Make sure you inform your trusted friends, ahead of time, of the intention and focus of your ceremony. Let them know about your process of connecting with the maiden within you, and about your intention to heal and celebrate her. Also be sure to communicate that the ceremony will be an opportunity for each of them, if they so choose, to tell the story of their own first Moon Blood, and to heal any pain associated with that time in their life. Let them know that they are invited primarily to bear witness, and to support your own healing, that their sharing of their stories in the process will be optional, and that they can decide about it when the time comes during the ceremony.

For this ceremony, you may incorporate all of the suggestions offered here, or you may choose to include only one or a few of them. Feel free to elaborate on a certain aspect and disregard others. You may also want to read other sample ceremonies in this book (such as "Our mothers' line" and "Welcoming girls into womanhood") and incorporate elements from those into your ceremony. These are guidelines, designed to inspire your creativity. Let yourself fly!

You will need:

- A simple altar: a space that focuses your attention and intention, placed either in the center of your circle (indoors/outside), or centrally around your circle (indoors/outdoors). Adorn it with objects that, to you, symbolize your femininity and beauty. These may include: a beautiful cloth, pictures of yourself as a young woman, images of other women or the Feminine, jewelry, statues, special objects or mementos that you cherish from your past or present life, a crystal or rock, flowers, other elements of nature, and so forth.
- A candle in a holder
- A garment that makes you feel strong, powerful, and beautiful when you wear it
- A bowl of water (preferably a beautiful bowl, but any kitchen bowl will do)
- A hand-held mirror

- A verbal confidentiality agreement to be established prior to starting the ceremony. (Refer to page 32.)
- A comfortable sitting arrangement, such as pillows, back-jacks, and the like. These could be provided by you, or by each participant (with advance notice).

Optional:
- Musical instruments
- A crown, tiara, or flower garland for you to wear
- Food to share (decadent desserts are a good idea!)

The ceremony
Let everyone arrive and settle; you will sense when it is time to start the ceremony.

The invocation
Invite the women to stand around the altar. If the altar is to be in the center of your group, have the women circle around it.

Light a candle on the altar to mark the beginning of the ceremony.

Start by welcoming everyone and stating your intention for this ceremony. Refer to the section of this book entitled "Elements of ceremony" (found on page 32) to choose an invocation that suits your needs, or, if you are comfortable doing so, create your own invocation.

The body of your ceremony

If the group is not already assembled in a circle, have them do so now and invite them to sit down. Once everyone is settled, with the bowl of water in front of you, start telling the story of your Menarche, your first menstrual period.

This may be the first time you have ever told this story, and it may be a painful one. It may carry with it a lot of feelings. Take your time. Know that the experience you are sharing is uniquely yours, yet in its essence it is intimately familiar to every woman in your circle and in the world.

Tears may surface for you and for other women around you. Let those tears become a cleansing stream with which you are washing off everything that doesn't serve you. When you have finished your story, immerse your hands in the bowl in front of you. Cup your palms and ceremonially pour water from one hand to the other, cleansing and letting go of all the pain associated with your Menarche, your first blood. With your hands still immersed in water, name out loud all that you are washing off. For example: "I wash off all shame associated with my blood. I let go of the scientific way my mother talked with me about my period. I let go of the idea that my blood is unclean in any way."

When you feel cleansed, pass the bowl to the woman on your right (as you may remember, counter-clockwise is a direction of releasing and letting go). If she chooses to speak, it is now her turn to tell the story of her Menarche, followed by a ceremonial washing of her hands. She may also choose to pass, or to ceremonially wash her hands in silence.

If strong emotions come up, encourage the group to silently witness the person who is experiencing them. Being *heard* and *witnessed* is often the most profound balm for a woman's pain. However, if you sense that the pain seems bottomless (which, in fact, I have never witnessed in the telling of the Menarche story) ask the woman experiencing it what she *needs* in order to have closure, at least for the time being. Recommend that she continue to pursue her path of healing the maiden within by finding a perceptive therapist.

Continue passing the bowl around the circle until all women have had a turn telling their first menstruation story, and have cleansed themselves of all that they no longer want to carry with them.

Take a quiet moment to allow yourself and the group to contemplate what has been released. Invite participants to remember that what they have released is *actually* gone, and that the only thing that can bring it back is a woman's own recollection of it. Instruct them that if a memory, or a behavior that has been released, comes up again for someone at any point in the future, it will be best if she immediately recalls the action of having washed it away in the water. For this will remind her psyche that the memory, or behavior, is no longer part of who she is today.

Cleansed and unburdened, the group is now ready for the heart of the ceremony: welcoming you into womanhood. Place yourself in the center of the circle, and let yourself be fully receptive as the Mistress of Ceremonies reads to you the words with which you have provided her, the words you wish you had heard at your Menarche. She may want to invite the rest of the group to follow her by repeating each of the phrases to you.

After the Mistress of Ceremonies has completed this recitation, it is now time for you to acknowledge yourself as Woman. Close your eyes and voice, internally, a statement that affirms yourself as a strong, powerful, beautiful woman in the world. This can be a spontaneous statement, or one that you have prepared ahead of time. Your statement may be something like: "I am Woman, rooted in Mother Earth. I am She who gives life and creates it. I am beauty and strength. I am hope. I find my way fearlessly, guided by my inner knowing. I am flowing with wisdom, my blood fertilizes the Earth." Create one that is meaningful to you.

Now, take a mirror in your hands, and, gazing into your own eyes, proclaim your affirmation out loud.

Invite your circle sisters to reflect your statements back to you after they are spoken, starting with the words: "You are ..."

Listen deeply. Let yourself move from powerfully affirming to fully receiving, and back again, as you speak and listen in turn.

If you so chose, music, songs, or chants would be a nice touch after all your statements have been spoken.

The closing

Please refer to the section of this book entitled "Elements of ceremony," starting on page 32, to find a way to close your circle, or create your own closing.

In order to fully complete the closing, remember to pour onto the Earth the water you used to wash off everything that doesn't serve you. As you do so, speak an intention, silently or out loud, that the water and all that has been released will fertilize new growth.

End the circle by thanking your trusted women friends, and have a feast!

III. From Healing to Mentoring

Mindfully modeling womanhood to girls

Only after healing the wounds of our own maidenhood can we model conscious womanhood to our girls.

Having delved into the memories of your own Coming of Age, having bravely met any pain associated with it, and having ceremonially worked on healing and celebrating the maiden within, you are well on your path to reclaiming your womanhood in its fullest. Now you will no doubt be freer to devote attention and intention to modeling such empowered womanhood to the girls in your midst.

This chapter opens the Mother-Daughter lens into the broader spectrum of Mentoring. It focuses on the advantages and freedom of assuming a Mentor or Elder role in relation

67

to a girl in your life who is not your daughter. It is intended for those who do not have daughters, as well as those who do and who might find meaning in mentoring other girls, as well.

When I lived in London in my late twenties, I had a close friendship with a colleague's daughter named Roni. We remained close from the time she was 9 years old until she turned 13, when I left England to come to the United States. I remember us drinking hot chocolate in cafes, going to the movies, and skipping hand-in-hand on the sidewalks on our way back home. This relationship warmed my heart, particularly because I had chosen not to have children at the time. I felt as if I had the best of both worlds: a close friendship with a child, and freedom from the responsibility of having to raise her.

In the West, our social structures are slowly evolving. Today, the nuclear family is becoming increasingly rare, giving way to blended families, extended families, and new kinds of arrangements and relationships in neighborhoods, co-housing associations, and other forms of community. Girls have access to a large number of adult women besides their birth mothers, and women have girls in their lives who are their heart children rather than their biological daughters.

These circumstances are placing a new and exciting responsibility upon us as women, that of **Eldering** -- becoming a conscious guide to young girls in our lives, regardless of their biological relationship to us.

When I started working with mothers and daughters, I opened my workshops to all women. I discovered that some of the most enthusiastic participants were the ones who arrived unaccompanied by a daughter or mother: mothers of boys who yearned to take part in an intimate female circle; girls whose mothers were unavailable or uninvolved in their physical and emotional lives; aunts; big sisters; grandmothers; and women who may not have had strong family ties but who had much to offer the next generations.

One of the most touching moments I remember was when an adult woman shared with her elderly mother the feelings she had experienced at the time she had started menstruating. These were feelings she had kept hidden for more than 20 years. The deep closeness that instantly formed as a result of that sharing connected not only the woman and her mother, but also both adult women and the sharer's young daughter. It marked a leap into a new level of intimacy among three generations.

Another deeply moving moment occurred at a different workshop between a teenage girl who had recently aborted an unwanted pregnancy, and a mother of two who had recently miscarried a desired pregnancy. The two, who had never met, found comfort and solace as they shared their stories and mourned together.

These experiences taught me how important it was to keep the circles open to all girls and women. The circles provided support for those who did not have an intimate connection to their mothers and for those who did not have daughters. In addition they allowed a bonding to take place between girls and women who weren't their biological mothers.

When an exercise called for participants to pair up with someone outside of their family, the results were profound. Girls found that they could easily confide in women who had not raised them. They had no expectations *from these women, and consequently could see and accept them for who they were. Similarly, women found it easy to open up to girls whose laundry was piling up in another mother's house!*

Something magical was happening: girls and women were meeting one another in an authentic, unencumbered, and creative way, and they were able to take that authenticity and freshness back to their relationships with their biological mothers or daughters.

Some girls, of course, already enjoy open, creative, and evolving relationships with their mothers. Yet some don't have a mother's presence in their lives. Some are estranged from their birth mothers, or are raised by grandparents or stepmothers. This is where aunts, older cousins, big sisters, mothers' best friends, or other adult women can step in and become mentoring elders.

Being a mentor can be enormously rewarding, and it is a role free of many of the complications and responsibilities that go along with biological parenthood. As a mentor, you choose the young girl you wish to model womanhood to, and develop a friendship with. You choose how much time you wish to spend with her and what kind of activities you want to do together. You can make the activities enjoyable and lighthearted, and you get to be yourself. In serving as a mentor, you model womanhood in an authentic way. While this, too, carries its own kind of responsibility, mentoring overall is pure fun. It is a wonderful way to be in a meaningful relationship with someone of the younger generation, to bring nurturing and inspiration into her life, and to experience the joy of unconditional -- that is to say, expectation-free -- love.

Biological mothers of daughters can also enjoy such freedoms by developing mentoring relationships with their daughter's girlfriends. To cultivate such relationships, you may want to have an intentional talk about the subject with the mothers of your daughter's friends. From there, you can arrange group outings, hikes, ceremonies, or other activities such as the ones suggested in the chapter "Circle activities for mothers and daughters, women and girls," starting on page 84. In those activities, have each mother devote time to pairing up with a girl who is not her daughter. A long-term mentoring relationship can grow from very simple and humble beginnings. You will no doubt come to cherish the carefree closeness that is sure to develop between you and your daughter's girlfriends, trusting that your own daughter is being similarly mentored by a woman you respect. Alternatively, a group of mothers and daughters may decide to switch mentoring partners each time they meet as a group, in order to give girls and women an opportunity to experience different flavors of mentoring.

It may be much easier to work toward a peer relationship *first* with a girl you mentor. You may then find that you can apply the insights and wisdom you have gained from such a process to the evolving relationship with your own daughter.

IV. Toward becoming Peers

A daily commitment

Girlhood lasts but a few years, from birth to Menarche. The journey of womanhood, however, takes a lifetime.

We know, when we birth our children, that we will be parents for life. Yet how conscious are we about letting go of our children with grace, at the important initiatory junctures in their lives, when they are called to independence and adulthood? And, if we don't have daughters, how can we help a girl in our midst -- a stepdaughter, niece, granddaughter, or a young friend -- to make this transition?

By preparing with your girl for her Rite of Passage into Menarche, you both ready yourselves for a pivotal point in both of your lives. This process is only the beginning of an ever-evolving journey toward becoming peers.

How is daily life going to be different for each of you, and for your relationship, after your girl's Menarche? At her Coming of Age ceremony, you will open a gateway for confiding in, and being vulnerable with, one another. This is a portal to a new, daily reality. Thus your preparations need to consider not only the details of this special ceremony, but also how they will facilitate the emergence of a new phase in your relationship, one that will continue to grow and evolve as long as you both live.

As your girl approaches puberty, take time, during your own moon flow, to sit quietly by yourself, and think about your daughter or girl. Let yourself remember her birth, her babyhood, her toddler years, her first experiences with school, and her growth throughout the years. Take as long as you need for this experience, which may involve more than one sitting.

Let yourself be immersed in loving memories of your girl's growing years. You may want to journal, draw, write poetry, or express yourself in any artistic form that feels satisfying.

When you are ready, start writing down all the ways in which your relationship with your girl is *un-equal*. For example: you are the one who is in charge of nourishing, driving, setting boundaries, and so forth. These kinds of inequalities may be a matter of necessity. Let your list grow from the black-and-white necessities into grayer areas. Are you doing for your girl things she is capable of doing herself? Are you getting input from her, and are you taking it into account? Are you giving her a chance to make some of her own decisions?

Take time, in your own quiet space, to contemplate and internally experiment with "What if ..." Ask yourself questions such as "What if I could feel a growing sense of confidence in my girl? What if I trusted her more? How would this look? How would it feel?" Allow yourself to sail on the waters of your imagination, trying on different ideas for size.

If you let this process evolve from one moon to the next, you will find yourself consciously preparing for your girl's Coming *of Age, fertilizing the ground for your relationship to blossom into new levels of trust and friendship.*

Mothers often complain that their daughters don't share anything with them. But how much do mothers share of their authentic selves with their daughters? At adolescence, a girl may confide more readily with a woman who is not her mother, yet to what degree does such a mentor reciprocate the confidence? Obviously, some aspects of your inner life are not age appropriate to share with a daughter or an adolescent girl. But I invite you to consider viewing your girl's Coming of Age as a time that launches a transition from your being her "pillar" to your being her friend. It is a time when you can begin relating to one another more as two adults and less as caregiver and dependent. Both of you will feel a measure of relief -- you will no longer have to hide your stresses or special joys from your girl in an effort to be the "rock," and she, in return, can let go of feeling "lesser than." Launching such a transition will start you both on an ever-evolving journey toward becoming peers while helping you to enhance the warmth and connection between you.

Being a friend to your girl is very different from engaging in a "role reversal" with her. You need to be sensitive about not burdening her with your concerns. Being a friend, and nurturing a growing peer relationship, does not mean leaning on your girl for advice or emotional support. For this, you will continue to have your women friends, or you will need to seek new adult friends. Perhaps you will even seek a guide, a mentor, or a therapist, to help you meet your own emotional needs. Becoming a friend and a peer to your girl means, primarily, that you start shifting your own inner perception of her as a child and develop a sense of her as an equal.

When weighing whether a given topic may be age appropriate to share with your girl, it will be helpful to remember how you were at her age. Asking yourself how it would have felt to have your mother share such information or topic with you, and paying attention to your emotional and bodily responses to this question, will give you clues as to whether to share the topic at this time. Themes that are generally appropriate for sharing include memories of your own questions and concerns when you were your girl's age; your feelings at the approach of your Menarche; moments of insight and revelation you experienced as a girl; thoughts of what you used to like about being a girl, and what was difficult; musings on what you came to like about being a woman or what you appreciate about your life. Your best guidance will come from your own inner adolescent girl.

A critical aspect of preparing for your girl's Rite of Passage is to begin cultivating this new, more mutual way of relating, well ahead of her Coming of Age ceremony. One effective way to do this is to establish a weekly "date" with your daughter or the girl you are mentoring. You may want to go out for tea, or stay home and be cozy. You may choose to go on a walk, a swim, or a hike. Whatever activity you do together, make sure your aim is to become close to one another in honest and reciprocal ways. The goal should not simply be for *her* to open up to *you*. (Look for specific ideas in the section "Circle activities for mothers and daughters, women and girls" on page 85.)

Prepare for your weekly outings ahead of time. Sift through all that is on your mind and heart, and decide what will be age appropriate for sharing, and what will not be. For example, it would not be appropriate to discuss your sexual life with your girl. But the story of your courtship with your partner or husband, of how you met and how you felt at the time, may be as deeply instructional for a budding woman as it could be satisfying for you to recall and share.

When I turned 18, my mother shifted her way of relating to me. I'm not sure if it was a conscious decision on her part, or an instinctive impulse. She died when I was 24, and the question about what had prompted the change didn't arise in time for me to ask her. What I clearly felt, however, was that she started talking with me as an equal at that time. She thus became my first real woman friend. I had peer girlfriends, yes, yet none of them possessed the life experience that my mom had. She talked with me about her childhood as an only child, growing up with a divorced mother. She spoke of her complex marriage to my father (mind you, I was over 18 and she obviously deemed me ready). She shared how her experiences had led her to decide not to subject her own two children to the life of a single-parent family, despite her personal unhappiness in her marriage. She admitted, *however, that she was thinking about ending her marriage once my brother and I were out of the house. I felt a sense of maturity and significance in being called to relate to my mother in this new way. At 18, I suddenly felt like an equal with her. Our relationship had evolved from a mother-daughter dynamic to one in which we were both adult women.*

This was profoundly healing, particularly given that I had grown up never feeling fully loved by my mother. In initiating the transition from parent to peer, she offered me a new level of loving and nurturing as a friend, which I had not experienced as a child. I still had to work out my ambivalent feelings toward her and come to forgive her for her mistakes (supported by years of psychotherapy), but I was, and still am, tremendously grateful for the adult years my mother and I shared. They both strengthened me personally and gave me a model to share with others.

Once you have begun relating to your girl in a new way by shifting your inner stance, and by setting up weekly dates, start thinking about how to integrate this new way of being into your life on an ongoing basis. The journey toward becoming peers is a *daily* commitment. There are many small acts you can engage in that will help this process along: confiding briefly with your girl on a challenge you are facing, giving her a loving hug, calling her from work just to check in, and generally adopting an attitude of equality by becoming willing to renounce rank. In doing so, you will be sowing the seeds of a friendship that may be the most rewarding one of your life.

Toward becoming Peers
Circle activities for mothers
and daughters, women and girls

To guide you in your work toward becoming peers with your girl, you will want to plan special activities that you carry out with her alone or in circle with other women and girls. These activities can be casual in nature, yet ought to be carried out with ceremonial intention. Ceremonial times are remarkable, for what you do in them reverberates throughout the rest of your life, like a pebble thrown into a pond.

The time you set apart to connect with your girl is _sacred time_. By setting an intention, and by marking the beginning and end of your time together, you elevate this time above the mundane and make it sacred.

When planning sacred activities with your girl, set your intentions carefully. These may include the intention to connect more deeply with her by cultivating more honest and authentic sharing between you; the intent to empower her as a budding young woman while empowering yourself and other participants as evolving wise women; the intent to affirm the feminine wisdom that flows through each of you by virtue of your cycles; and so forth. Setting a clear intention first will allow you to more effectively create activities that will give it form.

Many of the following ceremonial activities may be done at any place and time, not just in a circle, depending on how formal or casual you wish to be. You may carry out some of them, for example, while strolling in the park, driving in the car, or whenever and wherever you and your girl have a private moment. Again, your intention is what matters most in making your time together sacred!

If you choose to create a more formal circle of girls and women, you may use any of the following activities as the "body" of your ceremony. Refer to pages 33 and 40 for how to create an invocation and a closing, and to page 47 for creating an altar, if you chose to have one. Please remember to establish a confidentiality agreement prior to starting the ceremony.

Examples of ceremonial activities:

- Tell your girl (or the larger group) something personal about yourself that you would like them to know. Invite her/them to reciprocate.

• Tell your girl/group how you feel about being a woman, what you like about it and what you find challenging. Invite sharing and discussion.

• Tell your girl/group how your view of yourself as a woman has changed through the years. Pick an example of a defining moment in the creation of your identity as a woman, and share it with your girl/group. Invite a dialogue.

• Invite your girl/group to share what it means for her/them to be/become a woman.

• Sitting together, have each of you write an essay describing a day in your life 10 years from now. When you are finished, share your writing with each other.

• Sitting together, have each of you write about the woman you are dreaming of becoming. Describe what womanly qualities you wish to cultivate within yourself. Share what you have written with each other, and brainstorm ideas for how you may develop the traits you wish to incorporate into your lives.

• Sitting together, have each of you write about a female character (fictional or historical, living or not) who inspires you, or whom you see as a role model.

• Sitting together, have each of you write about what is it that you enjoy regarding your cyclical nature as women, and specifically, regarding your Moon Time. Include thoughts on what you find challenging about it. Share your writings and brainstorm on how you may lessen your challenges and increase your joy around your cyclicity and Moon Times.

• Create with your girl/group individual calendars devoted to your Moon Time. Use existing calendars as a template, or make your own. Let each person decide how she would like to mark the first day of her Moon Flow on the calendar. Be creative! Use paints, markers, stamps, stickers, glitter, whatever makes you smile. Decorate the first day, or the duration of your flow, monthly, on your calendars.

• Go through your closets and identify items of clothing and jewelry that are red/crimson, or that reflect your mood while menstruating. Create together a Moon Section in each of your closets, or in your jewelry boxes, where you group these items for wearing during your Moon Time.

• Share information about foods that you are experimenting with for soothing your system while you menstruate. You may want to have these goodies on hand to munch on during your time together.

• Make necklaces together for wearing during your Moon Flow.

• Make red pouches together for storing your special Moon Flow necklaces, other Moon Time jewelry, or your Moon Time hygiene products.

• If you use a bowl to soak your reusable Moon Time pads, make large red pouches together for containing your bowl. (See page 12 for discussion of how I made my own Moon Bowl pouch.)

- *Sculpt images in clay or in a commercial sculpting polymer that empower you as women. These could include images of the female body, or symbolic representations such as a bowl/well to represent your wisdom, a flower to represent your bloom, and so forth. Display your creations in a special place in your home/s during your Moon Time.*

- *Make your ceremonial time together be an official "Moon Time date" that you schedule to take place once during each of your cycles. Go out or stay in, and have whomever is menstruating talk about what is happening in her life during this cycle, how she is experiencing her Moon Flow this time around, and so forth. Celebrate with a yummy dinner or dessert.*

V. The Coming of Age Year

Calling our girls to accountability

Often, when women think of welcoming their girls into womanhood, they focus only on celebrating. Celebrating is indeed delightful! It serves as a way of honoring our daughters and girls in ways many of us have not been honored, and it marks a Rite of Passage, the doorway between their childhood and their womanhood. However, celebrating is only one part of the complex and ongoing task of becoming an adult.

Guidance must go hand in hand with celebration. Preparation for our girls' Menarche must include instruction through activities that will call them to new levels of responsibility and accountability. We are the ones who must show them the way into adulthood.

In most indigenous cultures, Menarche rites emphasize this element. Girls may spend anywhere from a few months to an entire year developing the inner strength and learning the activities that are associated with being Woman. In such traditions, when the day of Menarche celebration comes, young women are ready to truly leave childhood behind and live in an entirely new fashion.

This kind of education is largely missing in our culture -- for both girls and boys. Yet young people crave it so deeply that in the absence of healthy cultural customs set up to mark, honor, and help them move through their Coming of Age, they will create them on their own. And sometimes what they create does not serve their highest good -- witness the degree of alcohol and drug abuse, the premature experimentation with sexuality, the high rate of teen pregnancies, and the phenomenon of gangs, all of which are endemic among our young people today. These are all attempts by youth to mark their entry into adulthood, to fill in the gaps in a culture that by and large lacks proper initiatory rituals.

Thus, by lovingly setting tasks that will stretch our daughters and girls in preparation for their Coming of Age celebration, we provide them with opportunities for growth that are otherwise missing from our culture.

When our girls were young and learning how to ride a bike, we enhanced their sense of confidence by providing them with training wheels, which in time we removed, challenging them to maintain balance on their own. Our girls, like climbing vines, will thrive with a guiding trellis that trains them gently to grow in an optimal direction. What training wheels and trellises can we provide our girls at adolescence? The next chapter offers some specifics for how we may prepare our girls, throughout their Coming of Age year, to emerge as women when their big day comes, and beyond.

The Coming of Age Year
Coming of age undertakings

Girls' bodies provide a clear marker of womanhood: Menarche, the first menstruation. Yet the precise timing of this event is unpredictable. Girls' cycles can start as early as age 9 or as late as age 17. Most girls, however, start cycling somewhere between the ages of 11 and 14.

Not knowing exactly when your girl's menstrual period will arrive doesn't mean you should leave everything else to chance. Like garden plants that become "dangly" or shoot out in unexpected directions, our girls begin showing telltale signs of their impending womanhood through their physical and emotional growth. It is at this time that you want to begin to cultivate, nourish, and direct your girl's growth, so as to prepare her for a new station in her life. By designing a year-long process of instruction, you will be preparing her emotions, mind, and spirit for adulthood, for the gift and responsibility of being Woman.

Your girl may start cycling during your planned Coming of Age year, she may start after it concludes, or she may already be cycling now. The precise timing of her Menarche is not the critical factor here. The important thing is that she *undergo* the intentional journey that will take her, over time, from girlhood into womanhood.

I suggest, then, that you start planning for this process when you feel intuitively moved to do so. As you inwardly prepare, observe your girl for signs of growth and check in with your own instincts -- this will let you know when the time is right to initiate her Coming of Age year.

The tasks you will be creating and assigning to your girl need to center around preparing her for becoming an adult woman. This means they should help her develop a sense of responsibility, discernment, intuition, common sense, willingness to seek advice or help, self-esteem, and deep respect for self, others, and the Earth. You may want to add to this list any other qualities and capabilities that to you represent adulthood. Let your list guide you in designing the year-long journey for your daughter or the girl in your life.

Obviously, if the girl you are helping to initiate is not your daughter, you will want *to first discuss the process with her mother. If you and your girl's mother are good friends, this can open a new level of cooperation between you. If you are not friends with the girl's mother, you will want to obtain the mother's permission to have her daughter participate in a Coming of Age journey with you.*

Let your girl know that you are planning a journey of tasks for her Coming of Age year. Tell her she will have mentors along the way, and that you will be one of them. A good way to start such a conversation with your girl is by recalling your experiences when you came of age, any longing for guidance you may have had, or what you may be doing for yourself now to satisfy your own yearning for healing and honoring regarding your Menarche. It may be a good idea to solicit your girl's input as to which adults in her life she would wish to have as mentors. By speaking about your own adolescent journey, and by welcoming your girl's participation and ideas -- you will be piquing her curiosity and stimulating in her a desire to be involved. I have found this approach to be more effective than asking for a girl's permission to proceed, which merely sets up a role reversal in which the girl is "in charge," instead of contributing to the development of a reciprocal relationship.

As the designer of a girl's Coming of Age journey (whether you are the girl's mother or not) I strongly recommend that you initially gather a number of other committed adults (friends or family, women and men) to act as mentors to your girl on her journey. You will be one of her guides and the orchestrator of the journey. If you are not the girl's mother, you will want to include the mother in the process, if she's alive and available. The other adults you gather will become your girl's community of elders.

You will need to choose your girl's mentors carefully. They should understand the depth of responsibility entailed in this undertaking. They also must be willing to be generally available and responsive to your girl's calls or needs during her Coming of Age year.

You may want to start the process by first doing some initial planning by yourself, inviting people to join as you go along -- or you may decide to gather your group first and plan your girl's journey with them. Choose whichever option feels right to you.

Decide on starting and ending dates for the ceremonial year. You may decide to select full moons to mark the commencement and conclusion of the process, given that a woman's menstrual cycle has long been associated with the moon. This association is primarily rooted in the fact that both cycles take about 29.5 days; additionally, in the era before cultures used artificial lights, women apparently menstruated with the new (dark) moon, and ovulated with the full moon. Thus women cycled together with the cosmos and with one another.

You may also wish to have the journey last "a year and a day." This would follow an old Celtic tradition of initiation based on the 13 lunar cycles in a solar year, which take 365+1 days (a year and one day) to complete. Or you may pick other dates that work well for you and your girl (i.e., her birthday or another significant anniversary). Try to make whatever dates you select symbolically meaningful to you both.

Although a year is the ideal period of time for such a process, if you or your girl are restricted by your availability and cannot fulfill a full year's commitment, you may feel free to consider any time period ranging from six months to a year. It's more important that your girl have something rather than nothing, if you can't be available for the full year. If possible, however, aim for the full cycle of twelve months/thirteen moons.

In creating your girl's Coming of Age year make sure to design tasks that provide increasing levels of challenge, to be accomplished as the year progresses. They need not -- and perhaps should not -- be tasks that your girl can either "pass" or "fail." Rather, they should be activities that your girl can carry out in her own way, and that will leave her with a sense of accomplishment upon completion.

On the following pages, you will find sample tasks arranged in increasing levels of complexity. Their degree of challenge will differ from girl to girl -- order them in a way that makes sense to you. Whether you choose to have your girl do some or all of these activities, or whether you create your own, let yourself be guided by what feels natural to you. Aim for activities that will *create a rhythm that will carry you, as mother or mentor, as much as it will carry the young girl coming into her womanhood, through the journey of this year.*

The Coming Of Age Year
Sample tasks

The following Coming of Age tasks are designed to stretch your girl's abilities and will power; to expand her emotional range; to increase her capacity for critical thinking and decision making; to strengthen her sense of self-guidance; to build up her sense of accountability; and, finally, to develop in her an ethic of the importance of giving back to her community.

When you design or set her assignments, trust your girl to rise to the occasion. Let the task take her slightly beyond her comfort zone so that she can stretch and reach new heights.

Coming of Age is a guided journey. Thus your girl will no doubt best accomplish her tasks under the guidance of mentors. Assign one or more tasks to each mentor in your circle before you introduce them to your girl. Discuss the task with the mentor and make sure s/he feels comfortable and excited about undertaking it.

When you complete your list of tasks, estimate how long it would it take your girl to accomplish each one. Some, like growing bread from seed, will take more than a month; others may be completed overnight. Coordinate the timing of each task with the assigned mentor, and make sure to chart all of them on a yearly planner so you can space them comfortably apart.

The following list of tasks is meant to inspire you and tickle your imagination. Feel free to use any of them or to create your own, letting your heart and your intuition be your guide.

~ Keeping a journal

Keeping a journal throughout the Coming of Age year will allow your girl to develop perspective on her life, as well as document her extraordinary journey from girlhood to womanhood. Her journal, which needs to be kept private, will most likely serve as a close "companion," and may also become a treasured memento in her future.

Instruct your girl to find or purchase a blank book by herself. This independent step will symbolically set the stage for the rest of her journey. Encourage her to write at least one page every day, expressing her thoughts, emotions, actions, and hopes on her Coming of Age journey.

~ Passing on a childhood object

Invite your girl to choose one or more objects that were significant for her in her childhood years, and that she would be willing to part with. Encourage her to take time to contemplate the significance of the object(s) to her, and to then pass them on to a younger girl with whom she is close. She may want to share with the recipient (in person or in writing) what the object meant to her. She may also request that the girl pass the object on in similar fashion when the time is right.

~ Letting go of childhood

Ask your girl to choose one or more objects that symbolize her childhood to her. Invite her to artistically express (in writing/ drawing/painting/sculpting/collage or any other medium) the essence of her childhood as symbolized by that object. That is, she may artistically communicate themes such as why that object was special to her; why it, more than some of her other possessions, encapsulates her childhood; memories associated with the item; and so forth. She may, for example, choose to create a story, a play, a wall hanging, a 3D piece, a shield, or the like, incorporating her object into her art.

~ Fulfilling a childhood dream

This is an open invitation to have your girl fulfill a childhood dream, with the intention of closing the circle and saying goodbye to this period of her life. Invite her to develop a list of activities she has been dreaming of doing, emphasizing acts of maturity, not purchases. Then negotiate the selection and fulfillment of one activity that is both significant and fits with your budget, schedules, and so forth. This may, for example, be a particularly challenging hike or climb, a class, a camp, a special meal or activity together, a trip, and so forth.

~ Writing a poem

One doesn't have to be an experienced writer to write a poem. All that is needed is an emotional life, which we all possess by virtue of being human. Encourage your girl to write a poem about her transition from girlhood to womanhood; about leaving her childhood behind; about welcoming womanhood into her life; or about women (living or fictional) who inspired her throughout her childhood. The poem may be read at her Rite of Passage ceremony, if your girl feels comfortable doing so. It may also be given as a gift to someone special.

~ Keeping a dream journal

To help guide your girl's attention to her inner landscapes, with the aim of strengthening her intuitive capabilities, her inner listening skills, and her ability to access guidance from within, invite her to regularly record her dreams. For this, you may want to present her with a beautifully bound blank book as a gift. Have her keep it next to her bed, and suggest that she keep it absolutely private. This should be a separate book from her daily journal.

Her task is to write down at least one dream each morning before she gets out of bed, for a period of three to six months. This process can be facilitated by keeping her eyes closed for a few minutes on waking, while she recalls the dream's details. This will allow her to maintain maximum connection to the dream world, or "reenter" that space if her mind has already started functioning in daytime consciousness. She need not interpret or analyze her dreams, all she need do is record them. Invite her to periodically (monthly or seasonally) read through her journal and look for threads, themes, or patterns that may provide insights or wisdom about her life. At her Rite of Passage, your girl may choose to read, or tell, a particularly powerful or influential dream. Or she may want to talk about what she learned from the process of keeping a dream journal.

~ Giving thanks and making amends

Before your girl leaves childhood and transitions into adulthood, it is essential that she take stock of her relationships, express gratitude to those who have supported her, and make amends with those she may have hurt in some way.

To help her learn how to take responsibility for her actions, invite your girl to contemplate the nature and quality of her childhood relationships with each of her family members and friends. This process should take place over time, perhaps over a moon cycle (from new moon to new moon, or from full moon to full moon). Encourage your girl to write about her childhood relationships in her journal. She will want to contemplate the nurturing, encouraging, and supportive relationships in her life, as well as the more difficult ones.

At the end of this reflection and writing cycle, your girl will need to take a couple of weeks (say, from a new moon to the full moon) for reflecting and writing down an action plan regarding what she wishes to express to those who supported her, and how she will make amends to those she may have hurt. Remind her that with some people she may need or want to address both aspects.

The next step is for your girl to systematically carry out her plan over a specific time period. The exercise will help her develop a sense of both gratitude and responsibility for her relationships. It will assist her in seeing people through more adult eyes, allowing her to recognize that individuals and relationships may contain elements of the positive, the negative, and everything in between. It will also teach her that she possesses the tools to respond to each accordingly.

~ Exploring cultural images of womanhood

Have your girl spend a moon cycle observing, writing down, clipping images, or otherwise recording, all the messages -- overt and hidden -- that she is exposed to about femininity, femaleness, and what it means to be a woman today. Her examination should cover all forms of media (TV, radio, newspapers), popular songs, billboards, all forms of advertising, movies, school plays, all conversations (with peers and adults), books, and any other kind of information she may absorb. At first encourage her to simply be vigilant in *paying attention*, rather than evaluating and judging what she observes. During the data-collection period, she should be an impartial gatherer and chronicler of information.

After she has recorded her information, your girl should spend the next moon cycle examining the data with her mentor. Their task will be to now look at the data with a critical eye, extracting all of the messages about womanhood that are conveyed in -- and behind -- the images, words, and narratives she has observed. This activity will culminate with your girl writing a critique that describes how the "woman of our time" is expected to be, look, feel, think, and behave, according to what she has observed. She should discuss in this critique where, how, and why she agrees or disagrees with such messaging.

~ Creating an artistic representation of empowered womanhood

Having examined the cultural expectations regarding womanhood, your girl is ready to create her own original, authentic, and expansive picture of what it means to be a woman. With her mentor, she will look at her cultural findings and counter any negative, constricting, disempowering, or degrading images or messages about how women are expected to look, think, feel, talk, and behave with empowering, inspirational, expansive, and satisfying images and ideas. She will start by expressing these thoughts and ideas verbally and in writing, and will proceed to create an artistic collage to represent them visually. Her collage may include original or found drawings, paintings, clip art, 3D objects, poetry, song lyrics and music (of her own or created by others), and so forth. This collage may be displayed (and/or parts of it performed) at her Coming of Age ceremony.

~ Finding role models

Invite your girl to spend time with her mentor researching the lives of women, living or departed, who are inspiring role models of womanhood. She and her mentor may evolve a series of discussions in which they explore the lives and characteristics of these women, looking at what worked and what didn't work for them in their lives, and what she finds inspiring, moving, and stimulating about these individuals. The discussion should also consider what is a 'role model', and how can your girl apply the lessons she's learned from a role model in her own life.

If one or more of these inspiring women is still living, you may encourage your girl to set up an interview with her. She will need to ponder her intention for the interview, prepare questions, find the woman, and set up the appointment with her. Her task would culminate with writing an article describing her interview and the effect it had on her. The article could then be sent out for publication in a magazine or newspaper, or be made available for people to read at your girl's Rite of Passage ceremony.

~ Studying and practicing communication and conflict-resolution skills

We live in a culture that is quick to polarize and judge, but slow to resolve differences. Knowing how to communicate clearly, use language effectively to bridge divisions, and negotiate successfully so that everyone's needs may be met, are essential tools for creating and maintaining lasting and harmonious relationships. It is not too early to teach such skills to children at the elementary school level, yet schools rarely do so.

This task, then, aims at helping your girl to learn peacemaking skills. You may have her partake of one of the many classes and workshops available in this field. From NVC (Non Violent Communication) to PAIRS (Practical Application of Intimate Relationship Skills), resources near you may be found on the Internet and at community and youth centers.

If the girl you are mentoring is your own daughter, you may want to have the whole family partake in this activity with an eye toward improving communications and ensuring that everyone's emotional and physical needs are better met. (See the *Resources* section at the end of this book for suggestions on courses and organizations specializing in this field).

~ Making a garment

In creating a garment, your girl can choose her medium, such as sewing, knitting, weaving, and so forth. It doesn't matter how elaborate is the final product. The important thing is that she completes a functional, wearable piece of clothing that she has made from scratch. The garment may be kept aside and ceremonially worn for the first time at your girl's Rite of Passage ceremony. Or it may be made as a gift for someone dear, and presented to her or him ceremonially on the day of your girl's celebration.

~ Spending a night in nature

Most of us in the modern world to varying degrees have shut ourselves off from nature. Those of us living in the country may retain a closer connection to the natural world than those who live in an inner city, yet even in the countryside daily rhythms are largely human centered rather than nature focused. The activity of spending the night in nature is intended to help your girl gain a greater appreciation of the natural world.

With the help of an experienced guide, your girl may embark on a journey that will start with spending time in nature and studying its ways first hand. It will culminate with your girl camping out for the night in seclusion. She and her guide will choose a special site in nature where your girl will learn, over time, how to identify edible herbs, plants, and roots, recognize and imitate animal sounds, master the gathering of wood and the making of fire, and more. This immersion will turn the natural environment from an intimidating unknown into a reliable friend for her. The period of time you spend on this aspect of the activity will vary according to how long it takes for your girl to feel at ease in nature.

When both parties are confident about your girl's readiness, on a planned evening she will sojourn with her mentor out to an area that was pre-selected to be the guide station, where the mentor will spend the night. From there, your girl will walk by herself to the area previously established as her vigil site, which may be a cave, an open space, or a shelter (for a shelter, see the next task). She will carry water, a whistle, and a sleeping bag with her, but no food. The site should be located about 5-10 minutes walk from her guide's station. This will allow for her to be heard, if she needs to call or whistle for help, while also allowing her to maintain the solitude and privacy of her vigil. The purpose of this nighttime vigil is for your girl to enter into contemplation and communion with nature and with Self. She may decide in advance, or during the night, whether she wishes to include sleep as part of the experience, or whether she wishes to remain awake throughout the night.

During this vigil, your girl should have no distractions, no planned activities, and no "time fillers." The intention is for her to spend time in quiet contemplation, to face and overcome any fears that may arise as she sits alone in the dark of night, and to enter a state of deep listening for guidance from nature, as well as from within herself.

Your girl will thus need to prepare in advance a question or a theme on which she hopes to receive guidance during her vigil. This can be specific (such as asking for a spirit name), or general (such as asking for information that will help in her transition from girlhood to womanhood).

~ Building a shelter
Inviting your girl to build a shelter in nature is a further call for her to observe

natural rhythms, to develop an awareness of and respect for natural resources, and to practice the kind of self-reliance that indigenous peoples the world over have maintained in their interactions with nature.

With the help of an experienced guide who teaches her to observe and interact with nature (see "Spending a night in nature" above), your girl will learn to evaluate objects such as drift wood, fallen branches or trunks, large pieces of sea weed, boulders, and the like, for their usefulness in shelter building. Using a joining material such as a rope, and with her guide's help, she will embark on a journey of experimenting with the strength and insulating characteristics of found natural objects. This will culminate in her building a shelter that is warm and safe. The shelter should be sturdy, yet made of found natural materials only, which will decompose and, in time, return to Earth. It should be large enough to accommodate at least one person sleeping, or ideally, more than one. Once your girl has completed the structure, she may invite a friend, or a group of family and friends, to gather in it, spend time together, and possibly even sleep there.

~ Growing bread from seed

The task includes planting wheat (and/or other grains), tending the plants into maturity, harvesting the seeds, grinding the seeds into flour, and, finally, baking bread from that flour, which may be ceremonially presented, blessed, and shared in community.

This is an opportunity for your girl not only to tend to and observe the miracle of nature in creating food, but to also research and find out, in advance, all that is entailed. Questions such as whether you have the right climate for such a planting, at what time of year and where it should be done, how many seeds to plant, how much grain would produce a loaf of bread, what kind of care is required of the plants, and so forth, need to be researched by your girl, either through books or on the Internet, or by trial and error. Encourage her to walk in the shoes of her ancestors, and to be an adventurous explorer.

~ Giving back

Your girl has been sustained throughout her life by forces larger than herself. These may include her immediate family, extended family, friends of varying ages, teachers, school communities, after-school activities, youth centers, and the like. Invite your girl to make a list of all the people and organizations that played a role in her upbringing, either directly or indirectly. She should then choose two to five of these (people and/or organizations) for which she will design and carry out an act of "giving back."

Your girl may perform such giving-back acts alone (for instance: cooking a meal, cleaning a home, giving a talk, volunteering her time, and so forth); or she may initiate and fulfill them with a group of volunteers whom she recruits (for instance: planting a garden, clearing debris, organizing a trip, writing and performing a play, and so forth). The importance of this task should lie not in the size of the contribution your girl makes, but in the altruistic spirit with which she carries it out. She should approach it as an offering made out of gratitude for all that she has received in her life. No doubt she will also find that in giving, she will receive, as well.

~ Thinking globally, acting locally
Beyond her immediate community, the vast network of life, both visible and invisible, has also sustained your girl. Invite her to

write a list of everything that has been sustaining her life (such as the Earth, sun, water, air, plants, animals, minerals, and so forth). With the guidance of her mentor, your girl will then research the sustainability of each of these resources, and will choose one (or more) on which to focus her attention. She will proceed to investigate, design, and carry out an action plan for contributing to the sustainability of that resource. She may, for example, volunteer with an environmental organization, performing either hands-on work out in the field or in-house work, helping an office to function better.

Invite your girl to decide upon the length of her volunteering time. It should be proportionate to the level at which she herself has been sustained by the resources on which she has chosen to focus. Encourage her to keep a log of her volunteer activities and their affect on her. This can be used later as the basis for either an article or a presentation she gives to the community.

The Coming of Age Year
Welcoming girls into womanhood

Having explored your own maidenhood and the ways in which you were or weren't welcomed into womanhood; having felt the pain, mourned it, and let it go; having celebrated, as an adult woman, the Rite Of Passage that was missing from your youth, you are now ready to welcome your daughter, or a girl in your life, into womanhood.

Having accomplished some or all of the tasks you've set forth for her, and having cultivated greater adult sensibilities, your girl is now ready to be welcomed into womanhood in a meaningful way that fully honors her newly developed maturity. The following ceremony will provide the opportunity for you, your girl, and her community of female elders and friends to honor and celebrate this momentous transition.

A sample ceremony
This ceremony is intended to help you celebrate your girl's Menarche/Coming of Age. You may hold it when your girl starts menstruating, or, if she is already

menstruating, you may choose a good time for both of you and conduct it to mark the event retroactively. As you've already learned, it's never too late to honor one's Menarche!

For this special event, invite a group of women and adolescent girls whom your girl loves and trusts. You may have your girl develop the guest list, or you may compile it together. Instruct each guest to bring a gift in honor of your girl's Menarche.

As with all of the ceremonies in this book, you may wish to include all, some, or only one or two of the elements from this suggested outline in your own ceremony. Feel free to also read other sample ceremonies in this book (such as "Healing and celebrating the maiden within," found on page 53), and incorporate elements suggested there. What is offered here is intended as a guideline to inspire your own creativity. Let your juices flow!

You will need:

- A simple altar: a space that focuses your attention and intention, placed either in the center of your circle (inside/outside), or centrally around your circle (indoors/outdoors). Adorn it with objects chosen by your girl, which to her symbolize femininity and beauty. These may include: a beautiful cloth, pictures of your girl in varying stages of her growing up years, artistic images of women or the Feminine, jewelry, statues, special objects or mementoes that your girl cherishes, a crystal or rock, flowers, other elements of nature, and so forth.

- Special garments for you and your girl, which make each of you feel strong, powerful, and beautiful when you wear them.
- A candle in a holder
- A fireproof bowl (ceramic or metal)
- A plate (ceramic or glass)
- Matches or a lighter
- Thin pieces of paper about five to ten inches long (tissue or rice paper works well) and pens/pencils (enough for all participants)
- A bottle of essential oil with a fragrance your girl likes, and/or red paint (such as natural red pigment, water-based red paint, or red lipstick)
- A hand-held mirror
- A verbal confidentiality agreement to

be established prior to starting the ceremony (see page 32).
• A comfortable sitting arrangement, such as pillows, back-jacks and the like. These could be provided by you, or by each participant (with advance notice).

Optional:

• Musical instruments
• A crown, tiara, or flower garland for your girl
• Food to share (again, decadent desserts are a good idea!)

Order of ceremony
Let everyone arrive and settle. You will sense when it is time to start the ceremony.

The invocation
Invite the women to stand around the altar. If the altar is to be in the center of your group, have the women circle around it.

Light a candle on the altar to mark the beginning of the ceremony.

Start by welcoming everyone to your girl's Coming Of Age ceremony and stating your intention for it. Refer to the section of this book entitled "Elements of ceremony" (found on page 32) to choose an invocation that suits your needs, or, if you are comfortable doing so, create your own invocation.

The body of your ceremony

You may want to briefly share highlights from your own preparation process, sharing with the circle how your perspectives have shifted over time as your girl is transitioning from childhood to womanhood.

Speak about what "becoming a woman" means to you, and about your process of becoming a friend and a peer with your girl.

Tell the story of your first Moon Time, and invite others to follow you. Each woman may briefly relate the story of her own Menarche, or choose to pass without sharing.

When all of the stories have been told, take a moment to acknowledge the rainbow of women's emotions that have come forth. Give voice to the new level of intimacy and bonding that you all now share.

Pass the paper and pens around. Invite participants to write down all of the societal messages about womanhood that they wish to release, and any aspects of themselves they wish to let go of (such as self-judgment, fear, and so forth). These items will not be shared in the circle, so encourage participants to write for themselves.

When everyone is done writing, invite your girl to be the first to take the next step. Placing the fireproof bowl on a plate in the center of the circle, have her crumple her written paper into a ball, place it in the bowl, and set it on fire, using a match or a lighter.

While the paper is burning, instruct the circle to call out in unison: *"Be gone! Be gone! Be gone!"* until the paper is consumed. This usually creates a lot of excitement in the group. If the burning process takes some time and the group chant begins to grow slower, you may want to take the lead and lower your voice to a whisper; the group will follow you. When the burning paper is almost consumed, raise your voice again -- your next loud call of *"Be gone!"* will re-invigorate the chant.

Go around the circle as each individual takes a turn burning her paper and feeling the support of the group when she lets go of what no longer serves her. If the group is large, you may choose to have all of the participants throw their paper into the bowl together. Invite your girl to set fire to the pile, and have everyone chant while all the papers burn simultaneously.

When all papers have been burned to ashes, have the group take a quiet moment to contemplate what has been released. Invite every woman to remember that what she has released is *indeed* gone and that the only thing that can bring it back is her own recollection of it. Explain that if a released memory or behavior comes up at any point in the future, it will be best to immediately recall the flame having consumed it. For this will remind the psyche that the memory or behavior is no longer part of who the Self is today.

Clear the bowl to one side. After the ceremony, remember to pour the ashes on the ground around you (if you are outdoors), or out in your garden, in order to fertilize new growth. (Roses particularly like ashes!)

Now, invite your girl to stand in the middle of the circle and receive blessings from her heart circle.

As her mother or friend, you will be the first to bless her, and all others will follow you.

Approach your girl in the center of the circle. Using either essential oil or red paint, draw a symbol on her brow, anointing her while speaking your blessing to her.

[Essential oil and red paint are both equally powerful for use in a ceremonial context like this. Decide ahead of time which you will be using, and have everyone use it for the blessing. The red paint offers the advantage of visibility, and will allow for dramatic photographs. Essential oils offer the advantage of the power of scent, which can be used to create an evocative atmosphere.]

Have each participant take turns stepping into the center of the circle to bless, anoint, and present her gift to your girl.

When everyone is finished, hand a mirror to your girl at the center of the circle. Invite her to look at the reflection of her new Self. (Here is where the red paint will be particularly dramatic!). As she is gazing at herself, lead the circle in calling, three times, "Behold the powerful _____!" (Insert your girl's name.)

In this moment, you may wish to photograph your girl, who has now stepped over the threshold into womanhood.

The closing

Please refer to the "Closing" section in the "Elements of ceremony" chapter (found on page 40) to find a closing for your circle, or create your own. End the circle by thanking everyone who came, and conclude the celebration with a feast!

VI. If You Wish to Go Deeper...

Voyages to inner wellsprings:
Visualization as healing practice

In the ongoing work of empowering ourselves as women, it is essential to occasionally "voyage" inward to contact our inner wisdom, our ancestors, or our spiritual guides in order to receive nourishment and strength on a soul level. This chapter includes visualization activities that can serve either as a deepening of your own personal work (extending the healing of your inner maiden), as a complement to the circle work you are doing with your girl and other women in preparation for her Coming of Age, or as a way to expand your explorations once you have completed your girl's initiation. This chapter will first guide you in navigating a visualization activity yourself, and then will suggest ways for you to guide your girl or other women, either individually or in a circle.

First, a few words on why visualization-work is a significant way for nourishing and empowering yourself.

Some of the native languages around the world don't use separate words for "imagination" and "reality." They understand that everything our mind conceives is indeed reality. How can that be? Let's remember the example (on page 27) of the noise I hear in the middle of the night, which creates fear in me and sends adrenaline throughout my body. The realization that the noise is in fact a passing cat comes later. Yet the physical reaction -- based purely on an "imagined" reality, a mere thought -- has already taken place.

Thus thoughts are powerful originators of both emotional and physical responses, which amount to physical and emotional realities. Such internal realities can be generated in reaction to external events, or they can be created intentionally. Quantum physics has been affirming for the past few decades that our mind is indeed capable of generating reality purely through our thoughts. This knowledge is a powerful tool in the quest for human liberation from *suffering. For it means we have the capacity to shift our experience by shifting our thoughts. This is where visualization comes in. It is a tool for not only generating and shifting thoughts, but for creating fully fleshed-out internal experiences. Such experiences have the capacity to spill into our daily life and influence it in new directions.*

The experiences we have during guided visualization, then, like those we have during ceremony, are registered in our mind as reality. They will ripple out and affect our daily sense of self-esteem, worth, inner strength, and beauty. In other words, with visualization, we are potentially creating a more favorable world for ourselves. Our external reality will respond to match our new vision. (To find out more about how our thoughts create reality, you might want to check out films such as "Mindwalk" (USA, 1990), "What the Bleep Do We Know" (USA, 2004), and others in that vein).

This section of the book is an invitation to experiment with visualization as an extension of your work with ceremony. It is intended as a tool for accessing your inner wisdom, and the wisdom of the collective, for the purpose of healing and strengthening yourself. As you visualize healing and empowering spaces, acts, and encounters, you will be bringing healing, knowledge, and enjoyment into your life. You will find your daily reality beginning to respond by shifting in affirming ways.

It is best to begin the process of inward journeying by yourself. Once you are comfortable with it, you may want to invite your girl to join you. Later, you may even consider incorporating it into circle work with a group of girls and women.

As you enter into this work, keep in mind that in our "doing-ness" we are so unfamiliar with Being, that when all distractions are shut off, our mind may rebel. We may feel bored. But boredom is really nothing more than anxiety in the face of quiet. By staying present with yourself in the unfamiliar territory of inner silence, you will gradually grow roots deep in the fertile ground of your psyche. Slowly you will see shoots and leaves, flowers and fruit spring forth, nourished by the deep wellspring of your personal, as well as the collective, *female consciousness,* where the wisdom of the ancestors resides.

Accessing inner, deep, intuitive ancestral guidance is possible only in silence, in the dark, dreamy depths, not the bright light of everyday consciousness.

The journey to female consciousness, to your mothers' line, then, is dreamy work. To engage in it, you need to create a womb-like environment where you can switch off both external and internal noise. Turning off the ringer on the phone is only the preliminary step. Turning off your inner chatter is the actual start of the journey. As you enter into the silence of inner space, your thoughts may fire up arbitrary fragments of memory, "to-do" lists, hopes, concerns, judgments, reminders, and so forth. Learning how to calm such inner dialogue is part of the passage to awakening that will lead you into your inner depth.

Your random thoughts may surface time and again. It takes a continuing act of *will* to watch them and let them go, to observe them as you would leaves, floating on a surface of a rushing river. There is no need to catch them, analyze them, or focus on them. Over time, you will cultivate an inner equanimity that allows the leaves to float on the river's surface while you delve into your own depths.

If after you have begun a visualization journey you realize you have forgotten something, just let it go and don't disturb your flow. You will be able to do without whatever it is. If you find that a memory of a forgotten item keeps bothering you, use this as an opportunity to practice letting go of yet another leaf on the surface of the river of thoughts. See the thought floating downstream, and return to yourself.

Your intention here is to go inward with no agenda or expectations. You are merely opening to what you will find inside. Let any feelings you have simply surface and be, while you encounter silence, stillness, and your inner self. Breath deeply through any feelings, positive or negative, that may arise.

Preparing your environment

Set aside a leisurely period of time for this activity, at least an hour and possibly as much as two. Make sure you will have no distractions during this time. Switch off the ringer on your phone and any other electronic devices (radio, TV, cell phone, beeper, and so forth). Prepare an inviting place in which you may lie down. This may be your bed, a soft couch, a carpeted floor strewn with pillows, or your bathtub. It may also be a nurturing spot outdoors, in your own back yard, or somewhere in nature. The most important thing is that it be a place in which you feel comfortable and comforted.

Prepare any props that feel nurturing to you, such as candles, incense, scarves, or pillows. It is a good idea to have your journal nearby, so that you can write in it after your guided journey, if you are so moved. Avoid playing recorded music, however, as this comes from outside yourself, while your journey will be a process of going inward. In other words, you are getting ready to make your own internal music, and you want no distractions. Make sure you have everything you need set up before you start, including a glass or bottle of water if you think you may wish to drink.

Grounding

The following grounding exercise will serve as a good way to start any visualization or meditation. Read through it and become familiar enough with it to carry out the *steps on your own. Alternatively, you may want to record yourself reading this grounding exercise, followed by one of the suggested meditations. After you finish preparing your environment, you will be ready to switch on the recording, and relax into the guided journey. (If you decide to record yourself, start with the following paragraph).*

Close your eyes and focus on your breath, returning to it whenever you realize you have become distracted by thoughts.

Having settled into the quiet rhythm of your breathing, in your mind's eye see yourself in a quiet place in nature. This may be a place you have visited many times, or an imaginary spot that you are now seeing for the first time. If you are outdoors, visualize your immediate surroundings. Wherever your spot is -- it should feel extremely safe to you. This is a place in which none may enter unless you choose to invite them.

Shift your attention to your body. With your eyes closed and your breath ever deepening, sense which parts of your body are supported (by your seat, bed, tub, or the Earth). Breathe into these places, and release any muscular tension. Remember that Mother Earth, gravity, is ultimately supporting you; relax into her embrace.

Visualize roots growing from the soles of your feet (or any part of you that feels firmly planted on Earth). Sense your roots moving down through the ground beneath you, descending through layers of boulders and rocks, reaching to find underground waters. Drinking deeply, quench the thirst of your being.

Continue to allow your roots to descend through layers of dense matter to find the fiery core of Earth, the molten lava, the cauldron of transformation in Her center.

With your exhale, let go and release, through your roots, anything and everything that doesn't belong to this moment. Let it slide down your roots to drip into the core. Let it be transformed into pure energy by the fire at the center of Earth. Know that the energy you release is neither good nor bad; the Earth uses it for the good of all.

With your next inhale, draw up energy from the center of the Earth, through your roots, into your belly, your heart, your whole being. Breath in the freshness of this moment. Let your breathing be the only thing that exists now.

With your eyes closed, explore the place in nature to which you have mentally brought yourself. What is to your right? to your left? before and behind you? above and below? What does it physically feel like to be there? What smells or fragrances do you encounter? What do you hear? Are there birds singing? Are the leaves rustling? What is the temperature of the air on your skin? How firm or soft is the surface on which you are sitting or lying? Allow your senses to slowly drink in your surroundings as you continue to breathe deeply.

This is your sacred place, to which you may return whenever you wish to find comfort and solace, quiet and insight.

[Continue, seamlessly, with one of the following guided visualizations, or a visualization of your choice.]

Guided Visualization
Meeting your guide

[Continue, seamlessly, following "Grounding" above]

With your eyes closed, continue to notice everything around you. Allow your attention to be drawn to a slowly approaching female figure. Feel a sense of familiarity and anticipation as you instinctively realize she is coming for a dialogue with your soul.

As she approaches, see that she is older than you. Older, in fact, than time itself. Her presence feels comforting. Her eyes gaze deeply into yours. She extends both of her hands to you and clasps your palms in hers; warmth is slowly exchanged between you.

Without words, ask her for her guidance. Share with her anything that may be troubling you, and ask for solace. In silence, hear what she has to say... Absorb her wisdom by breathing it in through all the pores of your body.

Now, slowly, she places a gift in the palm of your left hand. She whispers its significance in your ear. This is the missing piece of information you have been waiting for. Listen deeply, and take it in.

Now you feel her gently holding your right hand and placing something in your right palm. Draw it to your heart and realize you have three seeds in your hand. Make a commitment to plant them, ceremonially, after she takes her leave.

In silence, she embraces you; she holds you in her arms for what seems like an eternity. Feel how safe you are in those arms. Mentally tell yourself that you may be cuddled by these arms any time you need it.

She whispers her name in your ear. You are the only one who knows it now, apart from her, and you know you will cherish this name for years to come. She invites you to call on her anytime you need comfort or guidance. Know that she will always answer your call, swiftly and warmly.

Reach in your heart and give her a gift of gratitude. What is this gift you are giving her? She smiles in acceptance. Touch your forehead to hers. She disappears in the next moment.

The seeds in your right palm are yearning for soil and water. With your eyes still closed, inwardly look around and find the perfect spot. In your vision, kneel on the ground, dig a hole with your bare hands, and prepare the soil for planting your intentions, as well as your seeds. When the hole is large enough, place your three seeds carefully in the center, bestowing each with a special blessing, assigning to each one an area in your life that you will nurture and grow.

Gently cover your seeds with soil and go to the nearby stream to fetch water.

As you pour water onto your seeds, soak them with your nurturing intentions and will them to grow. Bless their future root, stem, flower, and fruit.

Perceive these seeds as your newborn children. Make a commitment in this moment to nurture their growth.

Your task is done for now. Prepare to take leave of your sacred place by breathing in the beauty of it, knowing you will return.

With your eyes still closed, start bringing your attention to your physical body. See with your mind's eyes the physical place you are in right now. Remember the colors and shapes around you, and sense your position in the space. When you are ready, wiggle your fingers and toes gently to bring yourself into the present moment.

When you feel fully present, allow you eyes to gently open.

Guided Visualization
Women's mysteries

[Refer to the "Grounding" section, on page 135, to start your meditative journey.]

It is nighttime. You are walking slowly in a spacious forest, which spreads from mountains' slopes down to a valley. In that valley, a wide lake is nestled. Your feet are bare and Mother Earth, cool and moist, sustains every step you take. You feel grounded yet light. You are fully supported.

The night air is fresh and warm. Night owls and other birds converse among themselves. The full, round, yellow moon hangs low in the East, engulfing you with light. The sky is Her starry gown.

Approach the lake; the full moon's reflection lies still on the surface. Remove all of your clothes and enter the deep, slippery realm of Water. The first touch on your skin is cold! You feel alive in every cell of your being.

Swim toward the center. The soft sound of parting water surrounds you. Beyond that is silence. You are sustained in the waters of the Mother's womb.

The moon floats on the surface of the lake, slightly off center. Swim to enter Her reflection and bask in the light, breathing deeply. Feel her shining through your closed eyelids.

She now speaks to you from within. Hear her whisper: "Birth yourself anew. Give voice to the Wild Woman inside. Let her dance through your body! Let her sing in your voice! Let your movement be joy! Let your cells rejoice!"

Every bit of you is awake, bathing in moon waters.

Let the water caress you as you slowly swim to shore, cleansed and refreshed. Still naked, lie on the Mother's belly and feel comforted.

A warm, thick flow of menstrual blood begins to gently stream out of you and is absorbed by the body of Mother Earth. An inner murmur resounds within you: "The sacred blood of life connects me to all women, past, present and future; our flow is one, pulsing with the Earth. I am connected to them in a bond older than time itself."

Slowly women appear around you, circling the trees of the forest: women of all ages and colors, sizes and shapes. You all intuitively weave around one another in an ancient dance, led by your hearts and feet. Through your dance, receive the message they convey to you: "We are all part of an ever-turning cycle: waning and waxing, death and birth, darkness and fullness. As we spiral in a dance under the moon, we are connected by an infinite red thread."

A graceful old woman draws near. She leads you away from the dancing circle into the depths of the forest. You stop under a ray of moonlight and she faces you. Silently, she gives you instructions, and you grasp them with something *other* than your mind. Her words wash over you. An ancient part of you awakens; you feel a very old memory coming through. Reach between your legs and touch your blood; feel it, warm and friendly. Draw your red fingers toward your face. Look at your blood. Smell it and realize that it is odorless. See its rich color and texture. Touch your fingers to your tongue, and meet the salty taste of your insides.

The moon is right above you, glowing down on the sacredness of this moment. Slowly lift your hand and, with your blood, mark your forehead, breasts, belly, and feet. In front of you are the eyes of the Wise Woman guide who led you to the depth of this forest. As you see your reflection in those eyes, you both smile knowingly.

She raises her hand to bless you, and the women come back to you and gather around once more. The Wise One welcomes you into the circle of Women's Mysteries. She embraces you as her daughter. You now enter the ancient circle of women that is older than time.

You are Home.

In the circle around you everyone embraces: young and old, crones who now hold their blood and magic inside, girls who have just started bleeding, mothers and daughters, grandmothers and Amazons. You all begin to dance once more, letting your feet sink into Mother Earth. You howl to the moon. You sing to the Earth. You rejoice in your bodies and give voice to your souls.

The dancing peaks, then starts to slow down, and eventually comes to a stop. You now feast and laugh. The moon starts its descent to the west. It is almost morning.

As the first rays of the sun appear on the pale horizon, the women start disappearing one by one. The Wise One who guided you stays until last. You embrace in silence. You hear her voice inside you. She asks you to invite her counsel whenever you wish to talk or be guided.

You part without looking back.

You walk away from the lake, away from the forest, toward the city... Your steps are wide and light... You are going home, having given birth to the very old, and very new, you.

<u>Guided Visualization</u>
Guiding others

When you have experienced journeying inward and have become comfortable with the process, you may want to serve as a guide to your girl, or to a circle of girls and women. Visualization is essentially "adult work." Your girl becomes prepared for such work through the Coming of Age year and her Welcoming into Womanhood ceremony. Once she has crossed the threshold to womanhood, she stands at the beginning of a life-long journey. Visualization can be a powerful tool for this journey, and your initial guidance will lay the foundation for the work she may do individually in the years to come.

When inviting your girl to spend quiet time in guided visualizations, share with her the stories of your first attempts at it. Let her know what may have made you feel uncomfortable, restless, or bored, and how you overcame such challenges. Share with her, as well, the positive benefits that visualization has brought to your life.

Prepare her first journeying environment for her. Make it lush and inviting. Such *preparation is a gift in itself. You may even wish to offer her the first guided visualization as a special gift on a special day, such as her birthday or the start of one of her Moon Times.*

Unlike your own journeys, which you alone prepared (and perhaps tape recorded), your girl's first journey will take place in an area that is ready and waiting for her. She will be able to relax into the lull of your voice and fully give herself to the experience.

It is always recommended that you start any visualization with grounding (found on page 135). "Meeting Your Guide" (page 139) is a good first visualization. After you have guided your girl through the journey, let her know where you can be found, and leave the room for a time. This will allow her to stay with her experience and explore it in her own way. Subsequently, such inner work is best integrated inwardly and independently over time, perhaps through dreams, rather than through conversation. A good follow up to any inner work is journaling. Encourage your girl to spend time writing in her journal after her journey, even for a short while.

At a later time, if you feel a need to talk about the journey work, you may want to tell your girl about your first experiences of it. Your sharing may open the way for her to share her own experience with you, but that should not be your expectation. Allow her inner landscape to flourish in private, and offer yours only to the extent that it feels comfortable for you to share. Rather than sharing the details of any of your journeys, it may be much more rewarding for each of you to talk about the subtle or overt shifts you began to notice in your lives over time. It is not the specific details that matter, but rather the overall effect that journeying has on your lives that is important.

When attempting to guide a circle of women and girls in a journey, similar guidelines apply. Initially sharing the stories of your first attempts at visualization, what may have made you feel uncomfortable, what you are learning, or how you feel you are growing through this process (rather than sharing details of your journeys) will serve to put your circle participants at ease. When a few women in your circle have become experienced in journeying, you may want to take turns guiding the visualizations.

The visualizations in this book can be incorporated into any of the ceremonies described earlier. More visualizations are easy to find in other books (see the Recommended Reading section at the end of this book for some suggestions), and you can always try your hand at writing one yourself.

VII. Epilogue

Around the world: Cyclicity as a bond that transcends differences

A few years after awakening to the power, mystery, and beauty of my own menstrual flow, I started facilitating Red Moon circles to welcome girls into womanhood. Having witnessed age differences become insignificant as adolescent girls sat in circle with women of all ages, it occurred to me that I needed to travel back to Israel/Palestine, my country of origin, where so many issues seem to divide women across nationality lines, as well as within them. I wanted to form circles where Palestinian and Jewish women could sit together without experiencing barriers.

In January 1999, I traveled back to the Middle East to offer my first circle there since I had left in 1987. My Palestinian friend and former colleague, Nardin,[*] had graciously agreed to enlist Palestinian and Jewish women for my Red Moon circle -- which centered on a subject that was hard for women to talk about -- even though she had never experience such a circle herself. We knew and trusted one another from our days as co-workers with the Neveh Shalom/ Wahat Al Salaam School for Peace. For her willingness to take this chance, I will always be deeply grateful.

N.S.W.A.S. School for Peace, located in a village by the same name, is a place where Palestinian and Jewish youth and adults come to experience three-day reconciliation workshops. Located fifteen miles southwest of Jerusalem, it is still Nardin's home and the only Jewish-Palestinian village in Israel. Its name is Hebrew/Arabic for "Oasis Of Peace." It was there that Nardin and I had facilitated three-day co-ed workshops to assist Jews and Palestinians reconcile differences and come to terms with the profound political crisis in which they live.

---

[*] All names were changed to protect women's privacy. The names used were selected to accurately reflect each woman's nationality.

About halfway through the three-day workshop we would invite participants to divide between nationality lines, Jews in one room, Palestinians in another. There, they would share the pain and rage they were uncomfortable expressing in the presence of the "other."

At the time, the idea of dividing into gender groups never occurred to any of us. Our consciousness as group leaders, personally and collectively, was focused on the Israeli-Palestinian conflict. Gender didn't seem to be part of it, or so we thought. Yet over the years, conducting workshops for girls and women, I would often ask myself: What would it mean for Jewish and Palestinian women to meet in a sanctuary of their own, without the presence of men? How might this contribute to bridging the political divide between them?

Thanks to Nardin, twelve years after leaving Israel, where I grew up, lived, and worked, I was back at Neveh Shalom/Wahat Al Salaam. My Red Moon workshop for Jewish and Palestinian women would be the first gender-specific group offered there on this subject.

A crisp morning welcomed us as women started gathering in the hall where windows overlooked Jerusalem's pine-top ridges. The rolling green landscape dotted with wild flowers was familiar and reassuring.

Everything was coming back to me -- including the realization that numerous inequities can rear their heads in even the most well-meaning of environments. Take the name tags, for example. Some of them were being written in Hebrew, others in Arabic. This served as a reminder that while Arabs in Israel are obligated to study Hebrew from a very young age, Jews are allowed to remain comfortably illiterate in Arabic. This detail emphasized how issues of privilege and dominance can persist even down to the subtlest of levels. If Palestinian women wanted to be understood, they would have to write their name tags in both languages. Jewish women, on the other hand, would only need to use one language, their own. Embarrassed by my oversight, I blushingly asked Nardin to add my name in Arabic to my Hebrew name tag. This would be one way in which I could express my solidarity with all women present.

It was time to start our workshop. About twenty women gathered in the spacious hall, half of them Palestinian, the other half Jewish. A few, like Nardin, were residents of Neveh Shalom/Wahat Al Salaam; others came from all over the country. Most of them had never met each other, but they all knew Nardin. Nardin was pleasantly surprised to realize that, for her, this "summit" of sorts marked the convergence of circles of women with whom she interacted regularly in her assorted roles as mother, teacher, student, and village resident. Such women had never had a chance to meet, we all realized, largely because of the various kinds of social barriers between Palestinian and Jewish women, the very ones we were trying to help break down.

After a short grounding meditation, we started telling the stories of our Menarche, our first blood. The differences between and among us in terms of culture, religion, and economic status (of which all Jews and Palestinians are acutely aware whenever we meet), dissolved and disappeared. What emerged was a deep sense of commonality as we realized we all shared experiences and feelings such as embarrassment, shame, humiliation, ignorance, or fear regarding our first menstrual blood. No experience was unique to any one culture or religion. Essentially, we were all in this messy boat together!

Our work during that day continually revealed the bond between us as cycling women. Hidden behind the many faces of "difference" was the realization that we *all* bled monthly, we all had ambivalent or difficult relationships with our monthly flow (emotionally or physically) and we *all* had experienced transitions into womanhood that were far from ideal. Most of us, we found out, had been silent about these matters our whole lives.

Ya'el, a Jewish resident of the village, had brought her mother, who was visiting from the United States, to share in the workshop. "I have been living in this village for years, along with three of you women," said Ya'el to the circle at one point. "We are close friends, and we talk about everything. You, Dalit, even talked me into having children when I wouldn't hear of it. But I never, ever, told you this story of my blood." It was particularly moving for Ya'el to reveal to her mother how she had felt as a young girl at Menarche -- and to hear the story of her mother's first Moon Time, in turn.

Their presence in the circle as mother and daughter inspired a number of the women to resolve to have similar conversations with their own mothers. For those who had lost their mothers, their presence facilitated the ability to grieve that loss and mourn the fact that they would never be able to have the opportunity for such a conversation.

Throughout our day, in between the tears and the laughter, we sang and danced together. In preparation for the workshop, I had asked Nardin to translate the circle chant, "Earth my body/ Water my blood/ Air my breath/ and Fire my spirit" from English into Arabic. I had brought with me a Hebrew translation that had been made a number of years earlier by my Israeli friend and colleague, Carmellah.

As I taught the chant in all three languages, Hebrew, Arabic, and English, an array of emotions emerged within the group that once again reflected the political complexities of the Middle East. Ya'el's American mother and I were the only ones to sing in English, as no one else felt an affiliation with that language. The Jewish women sang in Hebrew only, as Arabic was too alien for them. The Palestinian women sang in Arabic only, although they could speak Hebrew well. The chant, which I envisioned would be beautifully woven in tri-lingual rounds, rotating from one language to another, turned out to be awkward. Suhair, my former Palestinian co-worker, later explained: "I can take speaking Hebrew all through the workshop. I can take speaking Hebrew most of my professional life. I can take doing all my errands in the city in Hebrew. But I can't take singing in Hebrew! This is the language of all the Israeli victory songs; it's the language of the military march songs, which are so popular in this country. I *cannot* sing in Hebrew."

In the awkwardness of the moment, a blind spot was revealed, and, with it, the raw wound that lay beneath. Suhair's anger and pain was evident, and so we talked and cried together. But mostly, we *listened,* until eventually everyone came to understand how it feels to be "other." This simple practice of "walking in each other's shoes" enabled us all to grow a bit more compassionate.

It was significant to observe that our bonding as cycling women co-existed in our circle *along* with cultural insensitivity. Having one didn't mean the other would automatically go away. While we had *discovered* our bond, we needed to consciously *cultivate* our sensitivity toward one another.

Uncovering our bond strengthened and deepened the motivation to become more sensitive to each other. Thus, as Palestinians and Jews, young and old, we had collectively reclaimed our unity as cycling women. This unity superseded such artificial divides as nationality, religion, age, belief system, and political bias. It connected us not only to one another, but to all women who had ever lived, and ever will live, on this planet, our Mother Earth.

At the end of the day, Nardin was exhausted, yet glowing. It was particularly important for me to hear her feedback, as she had worked so hard to make this workshop happen despite her busy life and her multiple commitments. "My life is full to the brim," she said, "but this day, which I have taken for myself alone, spent in the company of women from all walks of my life, connected me deeply to hidden parts of myself."

One desire the day had rekindled for her, Nardin revealed, was a long-repressed wish to learn how to belly dance. For years, she had ignored this yeaning because Israelis tend to look down on such quintessentially Arabic dance as "cheap" and "primitive." The day had stimulated in her, however, not only a pride in her womanhood, but a pride in her roots. She was going to find the time to belly dance!

My hope is that in your journey with this work, you, your girl, and your circle will similarly find renewed pride in who you are as individuals and women. I hope this book has helped stir in you the courage to explore new vistas, and has sparked the inspiration to make your lives as women meaningful, rich, and profound.

D. L., Sebastopol, California
Spring 2007

Resources

- **The Red Web Foundation** – *Creating life long menstrual health through community and education. A member-run, 501(c)3:*
- [*www.redwebfoundation.org*](www.redwebfoundation.org)

- **Museum of menstruation.** *A web site devoted to menstruation and selected topics of women's health:* **www.mum.org**

- **Center for Non-Violent Communication.** *Includes centers and trained facilitators worldwide:* **www.cnvc.org**

- **P.A.I.R.S.** *(Practical Application of Intimate Relationship skills). Includes centers and trained facilitators worldwide:* **www.pairs.com**

Recommended Reading

- *Circle of stones* by Judith Duerk. *LuraMedia, 1989*

- *Sister moon lodge* by Kisma Stepanich. *Llewellyn Publications, 1992*

- *An act of woman's power* by Kisma Stepanich. *Whitford Press, 1989*

- *Shakti woman* by Vicki Noble. *HarperSanFrancisco, 1991*

- *Dragontime* by Luisa Francia. *Ash Tree Publishing, 1991*

- *The red tent* by Anita Diamant. *Picador USA, 1997*

- *A time to celebrate: A celebration of a girl's first menstrual period* by Joan Morais. *Lua Publishing, 2003*

- *105 ways to celebrate menstruation* by Kami McBride. *Living Awareness Publications, 2004*

- *Cycles of life: A journal for women* by Kelly Mason, Elayne Doughty, and Ashley Ross (2007)

- *The wise wound* by Penelope Shuttle and Peter Redgrove. Grove Press, 1986

- *Grandmother moon* by Zsuzsanna Budapest. HarperSanFrancisco, 1991

- *When god was a woman* by Merlin Stone. Harcourt Brace Jovanovich, Publishers, 1976

- *Descent to the goddess* by Sylvia Brinton Perera. Inner City Books, 1981

- *The girl within* by Emily Hancock. Pandora Press, 1990

- *I close my eyes and see – Vision for the inner journey* by Dorothy Lewis. Findhorn Press, 1996

About the author

DeAnna L'am has been teaching in the United States and internationally since 1980 in the fields of team building, conflict resolution, peacemaking, and women's spirituality. She assists in building bridges across all perceived differences: between youth and adults, women and men, differing cultures and nationalities.

In 1994, DeAnna founded Red Moon Rites of Passage, an organization dedicated to welcoming girls into womanhood. It focuses on building bridges between girls and women of different upbringings, cultures, and beliefs -- through the use of ceremony.

Since founding Red Moon, DeAnna has been leading groups for girls and women throughout California and around the world. She was the first to bring Rites of Passage work to mixed groups of Jewish and Palestinian women in Israel/Palestine, which has helped women begin to find a common bond in their identity as cycling women.

As a child growing up in Israel, DeAnna's father used to tell her the story of "blue birds," which he said were a legendary symbol of happiness because they didn't exist anywhere. She now lives with her husband, daughter, and a small flock of ducks in Northern California, surrounded by Blue Jays.

DeAnna leads Coming Of Age workshops for girls and women, and creates personalized ceremonies to celebrate turning points in women's lives.

You can find out more about her work on her web site: _www.deannalam.com_

You may also reach her via email at: _lam@sonic.net_